C O N T E M P O R A R Y ' S

CHOICES
AN ESL LIFESKILLS SERIES FOR ADULTS
TEACHER'S GUIDE
FOR
- CONSUMER SENSE
- IN GOOD HEALTH
- FAMILIES AND SCHOOLS

CONTEMPORARY'S

CHOICES
AN ESL LIFESKILLS SERIES FOR ADULTS
TEACHER'S GUIDE
FOR
- CONSUMER SENSE
- IN GOOD HEALTH
- FAMILIES AND SCHOOLS

ELIZABETH CLAIRE   CAROLINE T. LINSE
MONA SCHERAGA   JANE YEDLIN

Project Editors
Julie Landau
Charlotte Ullman
Marietta Urban

CONTEMPORARY
BOOKS
CHICAGO

Choices: An ESL Lifeskills Series for Adults was developed for Contemporary Books
by **Quest Editorial Development, Inc.**

Published by Contemporary Books, Inc.
180 North Michigan Avenue, Chicago, Illinois 60601
Manufactured in the United States of America
International Standard Book Number: 0-8092-4045-9

Published simultaneously in Canada by
Fitzhenry & Whiteside
195 Allstate Parkway
Valleywood Business Park
Markham, Ontario L3R 4T8
Canada

Editorial Director
Caren Van Slyke

Editorial
Craig Bolt
Janice Bryant
Laura Larson
Lynn McEwan
Kathy Osmus
Cliff Wirt

Editorial Production Manager
Norma Fioretti

Production Editor
Marina Micari

Cover Design
Georgene Sainati

Interior photographs © C.C. Cain

Contents

Families and Schools 63

Introduction

Choices: An ESL Lifeskills Series for Adults is designed for ESL students who are at the intermediate level. Providing a student-centered approach to language learning, the *Choices* series features natural, purposeful language that adult students can put to immediate use in their daily lives. Language included is at both the informal and formal registers so that students will be able to function successfully in a variety of situations.

Choices will help students acquire the lifeskills competencies, language skills, and cultural information they need to make effective choices in the United States.

Format

The *Teacher's Guide* is divided into four sections. The first section, entitled **Teaching *Choices***, lists methods for presenting each section of each chapter and suggests general teaching strategies to supplement activities in the text.

The next three sections of this guide each consist of a Scope and Sequence chart and detailed lesson plans for each book. Each lesson plan includes instructional goals and teaching strategies. The activities included help students develop their listening, speaking, reading, and writing skills.

Teaching *Choices*

Each chapter in the student texts follows a consistent six-page format. A variety of teaching strategies is listed for each feature of each chapter. Your teaching strategies should be based on your students' needs, levels, and cultural and linguistic backgrounds as well as on your own teaching style.

Before You Listen

Each chapter opens with an illustration depicting a scene from the dialogue. The title of the dialogue, and of the chapter, is a line from the dialogue itself. Urge students not to look at the dialogue until it is introduced. The **Before You Listen** questions are designed to start students thinking about the topic of the chapter. Choose from the following teaching strategies:

- Have students look at the picture and guess what the characters are discussing or what is happening in the scene. Help students find details from the picture that indicate what is happening. For example, the moon in the sky indicates that it is nighttime.

- Ask students which character they think spoke the title line.

- Point out key vocabulary items in the picture. Have students identify other items.

- Ask students the questions or have them ask each other the questions. Encourage students to "prove" their answers with details from the picture.

- Have students try to figure out what is going on in the illustration by asking yes/no questions such as: "The people in the picture look angry. Are they fighting?"

Dialogue

The dialogues use functional language that students can apply to real-life situations. Present the dialogue using one or more of the following strategies:

- Read the dialogue aloud, changing your voice for each character.

- Read a line aloud and have students repeat it. Continue this procedure for the entire dialogue.

- Read the dialogue aloud with one or more of the advanced students in your class.

- Have students read the dialogue responsively. Divide students into the same number of groups as there are characters in the dialogue. Have each group read all of the lines for its character in unison.

- Many of the dialogues are open-ended and present a problem without a solution. These dialogues provide problem-posing opportunities. Have students work in small groups to come up with a conclusion to the dialogue and thereby a solution to the problem. Remind students that most problems have many possible solutions.

Words to Know

This vocabulary section includes words that are necessary for understanding the dialogue and are helpful additions to ESL students' vocabularies. Choose from the following vocabulary development strategies:

- Encourage students to try to figure out the meanings of unfamiliar words using the context of the dialogue.

- Present simple definitions for the words listed.

- Assign certain words to pairs of students and have them look up the word in a dictionary to provide the meaning and a sample sentence for the class.

- Have students look for additional unfamiliar words from the dialogue and write them on the lines provided.

- Have students create their own personal dictionaries of unfamiliar words. Address books work well for this purpose as the pages are already alphabetized.

- Have students play a vocabulary concentration game. Students write the words from the **Words to Know** section on one set of cards and a simple definition for each word on another set of cards. Students place all cards face down on a table. The first player turns over two cards. If the cards are a word and a matching definition, he or she keeps the cards and has another turn. If the cards do not match, they are put back in exactly the same place. The second player repeats the procedure. The game may be played by two to six players. The player with the most cards at the end of the game is the winner.

- Play the game "Team Tic-Tac-Toe" for an enjoyable way to learn the new vocabulary. Make a large tic-tac-toe grid on the board. In each square write a word from the **Words to Know** section. Each team chooses a word from

the grid and uses it correctly in a sentence. A correct use results in an X or an O in the square. An incorrect use gives the other team a turn. Continue this way until one team gets three squares in a row.

Another Way to Say It

This section features idiomatic expressions in American English. Choose from the following teaching strategies:

- Present the simple alternatives for each of the expressions listed.

- Have students locate the expression in the dialogue and think about why the speaker might have chosen the idiom over a more concrete word.

- Explain to students that figurative language is an important part of American life and culture.

- Point out which idioms are formal and informal. Explain when it is most appropriate to use each of the expressions.

- Read or have students read the dialogue again, replacing each of the expressions with the alternates listed in **Another Way to Say It**.

Talking It Over

Questions arising from the dialogue as well as questions exploring the general topic of the chapter are featured in this section. These questions follow a hierarchy of question types, beginning with comprehension questions to establish meaning and moving toward predicting, analyzing, and relating a situation similar to one's own experience. Choose from the following teaching strategies:

- Explain to students that not all of the questions have just one right answer. Encourage students to find all the possible answers.

- Teach students to determine which questions are asking for factual information and which ones are requesting an opinion.

- Use semantic maps to introduce vocabulary or lesson themes. For example, ask students what they think of when they hear the word *lease* and write the word in the middle of the board. As they call out words and concepts, write everything they say on the board in semantic clusters surrounding the word *lease*. In one area you may have the word *landlord*, surrounded by concepts that come to mind when that word is mentioned. In another area there might be prohibitions in a lease such as *no pets*, *no loud noise*, and *no washing machines*. Words that relate to the key word are clustered around the key word.

Working Together

Students are encouraged to explore further the language competencies in the conversation in this feature. Choose from the following teaching strategies:

- Present the problem or role-playing activity featured in this section. Model the language needed to complete the activity.

- If a conversation is called for, encourage students to experiment with the language needed to accomplish the goal of the conversation.

- Help students use words and phrases from the **Words to Know** and **Another Way to Say It** sections.

Real Talk

This feature consists of one brief note about informal spoken English.

- Explain that these pronunciation notes usually refer to the way people in the United States actually speak. Knowledge of this will aid student comprehension.

- Go over the pronunciation note with the students. Read examples or lists of words for students. If applicable, give students a few minutes to practice.

- Discuss briefly pronunciation variations which may occur in your region of the United States.

Putting It Together

This section includes a structure paradigm, a contextualized exercise, and a personalized exercise in which students use the structure to talk about their lives.

- Model several items in the exercise for the students or ask an advanced student to model for the class.

- Assign portions of this page for individual or pair classwork or for homework.

- Have students list their own responses to the personalized structure practice (*Practice B*) on a separate sheet of paper. Then collect the responses and put one of each student's responses on a class sheet. There may be fewer responses than students in the class because some answers may be identical. Make one copy of the class sheet for each student in the class. Then have students talk with each other, asking the questions to identify which of their classmates provided each response. For example, one student's answers to *"If you won the lottery, what would you buy?"* might be listed as:

  I would buy a new car. _____Juan_____
  I would buy a painting. _____Sumiko_____

Read and Think

The content reading on this page provides information that students can put to use immediately. In most readings key vocabulary items are underlined. However, when the reading is a realia item, such as a lease or a report card, key words are not underlined, as this could cause confusion. Choose from the following reading strategies:

- Show students how to determine the meanings of the underlined vocabulary words using contextual clues.

- Give students simple definitions only as a last resort.

- Read the passage aloud for students for the first few chapters. However, as the book and your students' skills progress, you may want students to read the passage themselves the first time.

- Collect samples of items related to the topic, such as product labels, school newsletters, or leases. Have students compare these items to those in the book.

- Call on individuals to answer the comprehension and extension questions following the **Read and Think** section.

- Have pairs of students ask each other the questions that follow the reading.

In Your Community

This activity encourages students to apply the information in the **Read and Think** reading to their own community and to practice question-asking competencies. This is an excellent time to bring in speakers from the community.

- Anticipate and model the language necessary to complete the activity.

- Have students work in a cooperative mode. For example, if there are five questions to be researched, students may work in five groups, obtain the answers, and share their findings with their class.

- Create a community guide for each community represented by your students. Compile into one volume all of the information students gather while using this section. Make sure that information includes addresses and telephone numbers. Duplicate the guide for each student to use as a practical community directory.

Figuring Out the U.S.

Pertinent cultural information related to the chapter topic is presented here as a brief reading or in the form of realia. Choose from the following reading strategies:

- Read the passage aloud or have one or more students read it.

- Have students identify and circle unfamiliar words. Help students determine if they need

to know the exact meaning of the words or if they can get the gist of the reading without the exact definitions.

- Help students make decisions about definitions based on contextual clues in the reading.

- Assign a paragraph to one or several students so that they can paraphrase it for the rest of the class.

- Encourage students to ask you questions about life in the United States and in your particular region of the country based on the reading. You may want to direct students to other resource people with particular knowledge of the topic.

- Encourage students to compare their traditions with those presented in the text.

Your Turn

This section allows students to "have the last say" in the chapter.

- Encourage students to answer the questions citing examples from the **Figuring Out the U.S.** section or from their personal lives.

- Have students create posters illustrating different opinions.

- Discuss variations from country to country as well as variations within each country and within the United States.

- Set up a panel discussion similar to talk shows on television with different students representing different points of view.

- Plan a real-life writing exercise based on information discussed in the **Figuring Out the U.S.** section.

- Have students reread the **Your Turn** questions. Ask students whether or not each question would make a good writing topic. Have students give reasons for their choices.

- Semantic maps, described on page 3 of this guide, can also be used to help students organize their ideas for writing activities.

Before they begin to write, they can jot down their ideas on a semantic map. Each cluster of items may be the basis for a paragraph.

Review Units

After every three chapters there is an interactive learning review for students to practice lifeskills competencies and/or review vocabulary. These are information-gap activities: students work in pairs. Each person has information that his or her partner does not have. Students work together to complete the activity.

- Try pairing more advanced students with those who need extra practice.

- Point out that students should look at their assigned page only. Peeking at the other page will ruin the fun and the exercise.

- Have pairs of students compare their answers in a class session.

Specific review unit teaching suggestions for *Consumer Sense*, *In Good Health*, and *Families and Schools* are found on pages 34, 62, and 90, respectively.

Using the Lesson Plans

Specific page-by-page teaching suggestions for *Consumer Sense*, *In Good Health*, and *Families and Schools* begin on pages 7, 35, and 63, respectively. The lesson plan for each chapter of the student text is two pages in length.

A summary of each chapter is given at the beginning of each lesson plan for quick identification. *Competency* refers to the lifeskills competency (or competencies) featured in the lesson. *Content Reading* identifies the **Read and Think** topic. *Cultural Reading* identifies the **Figuring Out the U.S.** topic. *Structure* lists the grammatical concept covered in **Putting It Together**. *Listening/Speaking Tip* refers to the **Real Talk** topic.

Each lesson plan contains a wide variety of strategies that may be used to initiate discussions as well as role-playing. There are also numerous suggestions—such as bringing in guest speakers and having students visit community agencies—to help bridge the gap between the classroom and the community.

Language acquisition is enhanced when students are actively and cheerfully engaged in the learning. Some groups of students will find writing activities enjoyable, while others will prefer role-playing. Select activities that your students will enjoy and benefit from most.

CONSUMER SENSE

MONA SCHERAGA

Scope and Sequence

CHAPTER	COMPETENCIES	
Chapter 1 For Rent	• Negotiating with a landlord • Interpreting lease and rental agreements	• Interpreting information about the rights of a renter and the rights of a landlord
Chapter 2 Filling the Refrigerator	• Interpreting food packaging labels	• Interpreting information or directions to locate consumer goods
Chapter 3 This Supermarket Is Expensive!	• Comparing food prices • Using coupons to purchase goods and services	• Interpreting labels to select goods and services
Chapter 4 We Would Like a Phone	• Interpreting information about obtaining a telephone	• Interpreting telephone rates and procedures
Chapter 5 But We Did Pay It!	• Understanding telephone bills • Using the telephone directory and related publications to locate information	• Interpreting information about time zones
Chapter 6 It's Fun to Eat Out	• Identifying methods used to purchase goods and services	• Interpreting restaurant menus and computing related costs
Chapter 7 It's a Luxury We Can't Afford	• Interpreting information about personal and family budgets	• Interpreting credit applications and recognizing how to use and maintain credit
Chapter 8 How Do We Get There?	• Asking for, giving, and following directions	• Using maps related to travel needs
Chapter 9 May I Help You?	• Returning/exchanging a purchase • Comparing prices or quality to determine the best buys for goods and services	• Interpreting clothing-care labels
Chapter 10 I'm Busy Right Now	• Dealing with telephone solicitations	• Identifying methods used to purchase goods and services
Chapter 11 I Want to Think It Over	• Interpreting information related to the selection and purchase of a car	• Planning for major purchases
Chapter 12 That Makes Sense	• Interpreting procedures associated with banking services	• Demonstrating use of savings and checking accounts

Consumer Sense

CONTENT READING	CULTURAL READING	STRUCTURE
A lease	Tenants, landlords, and leases	Contractions
Lists of ingredients	Shopping in supermarkets or neighborhood stores	*Some/Any*
Food ads	American advertisements	Comparisons
A telephone rate chart	Answering-machine messages	Present perfect
A telephone bill	Telephone customs	*Should/Shouldn't*
Menus	Eating in restaurants	Superlatives
A credit card statement	Budgeting	*Would like*
A map to a garage sale	Shopping malls	Embedded questions
Clothing labels	Salesclerks in the U.S.	*If/Then* statements
A warranty	Hunting for bargains	*Could* or *would/Can* or *will*
Car ads	Driving in the U.S.	Wh-questions
A check and checkbook	Using automatic teller cards	Time phrases

1 For Rent

Competency
Negotiating with a landlord

Content Reading
A lease

Cultural Reading
Tenants, landlords, and leases

Structure
Contractions

Listening/Speaking Tip
Going to/"Gonna"

Before You Listen (Page 1)

1. Introduce the illustration using the strategies on page 1 of this guide. Ask questions about the picture, such as: "What do you think the people are doing? What is on the floor?" Encourage students to talk about what they see in the picture.

2. Teach key vocabulary such as *rent*, *apartment*, *landlord*, *neighbors*, and *mess*. Encourage students to ask about any vocabulary items that are indicated in the picture.

Dialogue (Page 2)

1. Present the dialogue orally, choosing from the strategies on page 1 of this guide.

2. After students have heard the dialogue twice, check their comprehension with questions such as: "Is the rent $500 or $5,000? What is Nilda's roommate's name?"

3. Students may read the dialogue aloud in pairs, taking the roles of Nilda and the landlord and then switching roles so that each student reads each part.

Talking It Over (Page 3)

1. If you have ever negotiated with a landlord, share your experiences with students. Ask about their experiences with landlords.

2. Make a chart of yes/no questions based on questions 4, 5, and 6 on page 3 of the student text and any other questions that arise in the discussion. Put the chart on the board and talk as a group about students' experiences.

Working Together (Page 3)

1. Ask students if they have ever rented an apartment. If any have, ask them what questions they asked the landlord. Suggest questions such as: "Are children allowed? Are pets allowed? Is there public transportation or parking nearby? Are the neighbors quiet?" List their ideas on the board.

2. Write the sample conversation on the board and ask students, "What question would you ask next? How might the landlord answer?" Write the conversation they compose on the board and have them practice it in pairs.

3. After they have mastered the conversation, ask for two volunteers to present it to the class.

4. Encourage students to compose their own conversations based on the one they composed in class. Have students practice them in pairs and present them to the class.

Real Talk (Page 3)

Explain that students will hear people say words such as *gonna* and other comparable structures, but that they should always write *going to*. Have students work orally in pairs and practice creating sentences with *gonna* and *going to*.

Putting It Together (Page 4)

1. Explain that contractions are two words made into one word with an apostrophe (') replacing the missing letters. It is also important to note that contractions are not always appropriate. For example, the response to the question "Are you coming with us?" is not "I'm" but "I am"; however, a contraction can be used in the negative: "I'm not." In very short sentences, the long form is generally preferred. Explain that "I will not" becomes "I won't." Introduce any other relevant contractions.

2. *Practice A* can be presented either as a writing or a listening exercise. If it is a writing exercise, students can fill in the blanks using the words in bold. If it is a listening exercise, you can read the conversation using some contractions and some long forms.

3. Before students begin *Practice B*, brainstorm with them about vocabulary words that relate to apartments. Write the words they come up with on the board. Have them discuss with a partner what they can or can't do where they live. It may be helpful to make a list on the board of what they can or can't do so they can compare their situations to those of their classmates.

Read and Think (Page 5)

1. Refer to the reading strategies on page 3 of this guide. You may want to introduce the **Figuring Out the U.S.** reading on page 6 of the student text before introducing the lease.

2. Encourage the students to ask questions about the lease. Ask them questions to check comprehension, such as: "What do you think it means to *comply with the terms of the lease*?" or "What does *the ending date of the term* mean?" After the class has shown that they understand the lease, ask them questions such as: "Do you think the lease is fair to the landlord and to the tenant?"

3. If the lease in the student text is not similar to the standard lease used in your community, bring in a copy of the lease that is most commonly used and discuss it with students.

In Your Community (Page 5)

1. Plan a class trip to a tenants' rights organization and/or a governmental agency that deals with tenant-landlord issues. Have students make a list of questions beforehand to ask the representatives of these organizations.

2. Another option is to bring in speakers such as a representative from a tenants' rights organization or a lawyer who specializes in tenant-landlord agreements. Have students make a list of questions beforehand to ask the speaker. Be sure they write a class thank-you note afterward.

3. If the options suggested in numbers 1 and 2 in this section are not possible, bring in information from the organizations mentioned. It may be helpful for the students to role-play the parts of people who work in tenants' rights organizations and those of people looking for information.

Figuring Out the U.S. (Page 6)

Discuss tenant-landlord issues—rent control, for example—in your community.

Your Turn (Page 6)

Discuss the questions as a group. Have students write about questions 4 or 5 or have them document a problem (real or imagined) for a landlord. For example:

| 3/16 | 3:00 A.M. | Neighbors turned on loud music. |
| 3/16 | 3:15 A.M. | Asked neighbors to turn down music. They refused. |

Explain that they should write the date, the time, and their version of what happened. After you review their work, ask volunteers to read their documented problems to the class.

2 Filling the Refrigerator

Before You Listen (Page 7)

1. Introduce the illustration using the strategies on page 1 of this guide. Ask questions about the picture, such as: "Where do you think Kim and Nilda are? Why do you think the number 3 is on the sign? What do you think Nilda is pointing to?" Encourage students to describe what they see in the picture.

2. Teach key vocabulary such as *quantity*, *label*, *ingredients*, and *product*. Encourage students to ask about any vocabulary items that are indicated in the picture.

Dialogue (Page 8)

1. Present the dialogue orally, choosing from the strategies on page 1 of this guide.

2. After students have heard the dialogue twice, check their comprehension with questions such as: "Which is more expensive, meat-flavored sauce or sauce with real meat in it? Where is the milk?"

3. Students may read the dialogue aloud in pairs, taking the roles of Kim and Nilda and then switching roles so that each student reads each part.

Talking It Over (Page 9)

1. Bring in some food items with labels or ask students to bring in some items with labels for class discussion. Together, make a list of

the kinds of information found on labels, such as ingredients, weight, nutritional information, and directions for cooking. Discuss words or abbreviations students are not sure of, such as RDA (recommended daily allowance).

2. Have students work in pairs or groups to create a label for a product of their choice. Be sure they include all necessary information (see number 1 in this section). Have them create the labels on poster paper for display and discussion.

3. Talk about any ingredients students don't understand. Ask if they know what *preservatives* are. Explain what flavorings and additives are. If appropriate, talk about food allergies, especially to ingredients such as MSG (monosodium glutamate).

Working Together (Page 9)

1. Be sure you pair people with different partners as often as possible, so each person has an opportunity to work with all the students in the class. As students work in pairs, circulate and help those who are having trouble getting started. Have students practice the conversations they've created and have volunteers present them to the class. If you have trouble getting volunteers to begin, be one yourself. Work with students and ad-lib so they see how easy it can be.

2. Together, make a list of other questions you might ask in a supermarket. Have volunteers ask and answer the questions.

3. Discuss what to do if you don't find answers to your questions. Introduce language such as: "May I speak to the manager, please?" or "I'd like to speak to the person in charge, please."

Real Talk (Page 9)

1. Tell students to listen to your questions, not to answer them. Have them notice whether your voice rises or falls at the end of each question. Model questions such as: "Does my voice rise or fall at the end of each one? Do

you have any food allergies? Do you always read food labels? Where do you shop for food? Which is cheaper, an item with real fruit or one that has fruit flavoring?" You might want to diagram intonation like this:

Where do /you⌐ shop for food?

2. Put students in groups and have each group write two questions that require a yes/no response and two wh-questions, all of them on separate strips of paper. Put the strips in a paper bag and have each student reach in and pick one to read to the class. Make a note to work individually with any students who have a problem with the right stress and intonation.

Putting It Together (Page 10)

1. After introducing the paradigm, ask the students meaningful questions using *any*, such as: "Do you have *any* money to lend me?" Write their positive and negative responses on the board.

2. Put the words below on the board. Ask students to make sentences or questions about the classroom using the following words with *some* or *any*:
(Example: *There are* some *windows in the classroom.*)
men children lights leases
women pencils dogs television sets

3. In *Practice A*, give the students an example using *any* such as: "Is Kim buying *any* tissues?" Call on different students to ask and answer questions about the picture.

4. Model a shopping list on the board for *Practice B*. Have students work in pairs using the dialogue as a model to create shopping lists. Tell them to exchange shopping lists and check them for accuracy. Did they put in too many items or leave out any important ones? For example, if Person A said he didn't need any lettuce, Person B should not have written *lettuce* on the list.

Read and Think (Page 11)

You can have students answer questions 1 through 10 in a class discussion or, for variety, you can set up two teams: if no one on team 1 knows the answer to the first question, team 2 gets a chance to answer, and vice versa. Provide small prizes for the team with the most correct answers.

In Your Community (Page 11)

Have students decide beforehand which items they want to check and where they want to check them so there will be a variety of perishables and stores. Help them make a simple chart—like the following—before they go:

Date of Visit	Store Name	Item	Exp. Date of item in front	Exp. Date of item in back

Figuring Out the U.S. (Page 12)

1. Ask questions such as: "Do you shop differently now from the way you shopped in your native country? If so, how?" Encourage them to discuss their experiences shopping for food in the United States.

2. Ask about what kinds of things people can find in neighborhood stores that they might not find in supermarkets. Ask students why they think this is so.

Your Turn (Page 12)

1. Have several pairs role-play question 3. Discuss different ways of handling such situations.

2. Have students make a list of ways to shop for food in the United States. Some examples are supermarkets, farmers' markets, or convenience stores. Have dictionaries available or write out words the students have trouble spelling.

3 This Supermarket Is Expensive!

> **Competency**
> Comparing food prices
>
> **Content Reading**
> Food ads
>
> **Cultural Reading**
> American advertisements
>
> **Structure**
> Comparisons
>
> **Listening/Speaking Tip**
> -s endings

Before You Listen (Page 13)

1. Introduce the illustration using the strategies on page 1 of this guide. Have students ask each other questions based on the picture. Ask, "What is the cashier doing? Why do you think Nilda is watching the cashier?"

2. Teach key vocabulary such as *cashier, expensive, cheap, sale,* and *brand.* Encourage students to ask about any vocabulary items that are indicated in the picture.

Dialogue (Page 14)

1. Present the dialogue orally, choosing from the strategies on page 1 of this guide.

2. After students have heard the dialogue twice, check their comprehension with questions such as: "Are store brands cheaper or more expensive than name brands? Was the orange juice $2.19 or $1.89?"

3. Students may read the dialogue aloud in pairs, taking the roles of Nilda and the cashier and then switching roles so that each student reads each part.

Talking It Over (Page 15)

1. After you have discussed the questions in the student text, talk about brand names and store brands, explaining that many name brands are also packed under store brand labels. Explain that fruits and vegetables, for example, may be packed under the grower's name and also under five or six different supermarket labels. Ask if students are loyal to particular brands and why.

2. If you have students who use shopping lists, ask if they buy only what's on their shopping lists. Talk about the advice to consumers that they should never go shopping when they're hungry. Ask, "Why do you think this advice is given?"

Working Together (Page 15)

Pair students and give each pair a different occasion for which to shop, such as a party or the setting up of a new apartment. Tell them exactly how much money they have to spend. Have them present their situation and their lists to the class. If you have students who don't normally do the grocery shopping, be sure to pair them with students who do.

Real Talk (Page 15)

1. After your students practice saying the words, have them close their books. Write the words on the board in random order and have various students pronounce them.

2. Talk to your students about voiced and voiceless sounds. You may want to use the following chart:

Voiced Sounds										
g	dg	b	d	l	m	n	r	th	v	z
log	judge	grab	pad	pull	dam	den	pair	the	give	fuzz

Voiceless Sounds							
ch	k	f	p	s	t	sh	th
teach	pack	half	top	pass	hat	push	thank

Tell students to put their fingertips on their vocal cords and have them pronounce the words. They should feel their vocal cords vibrate when they say words with the voiced sounds, but they shouldn't feel any vibrations when they say the words with the voiceless sounds.

3. Go through the list on the board again, covering the final s on the words. Have the class say each word, fingertips on throat.

Putting It Together (Page 16)

1. Teach irregular comparatives *good/better, bad/worse, far/farther*, writing them on the board to show spellings. Use your students and items in the room for comparisons. For example: "Who comes from farther away, José or Ibraham? Which is easier, speaking English or writing English?" Have them create their own sentences with comparisons.

2. *Practice A* can be presented either as a writing or a speaking exercise. If it is to be a writing exercise, students can fill in the blanks with the correct comparison. If it is to be a speaking exercise, have students work in pairs and present the dialogue to the class. Make a list on the board of the various comparisons used. Talk about synonyms students may have used, such as *nearer* and *closer*.

3. In *Practice B*, create an example together on the board and suggest other comparisons, such as *close, far (farther), small, roomy, good (better),* and *bad (worse).* Have students work in pairs, writing down their comparisons in order to remember them and to practice the written form. Ask how many compared the same stores and whether their opinions were the same.

Read and Think (Page 17)

1. Discuss the ads in the student text with the class. Encourage comparison of the two stores, using models from *Practice B* in **Putting It Together.** Review the fine print. Have students work in pairs and ask each other questions 1 to 7.

2. Bring in newspaper ads from different stores in the area and have students do so, too. Let them work in pairs to compare prices of the same items in two different stores, compare the prices of items with and without coupons, and note specific directions on various coupon items (restrictions, expiration dates). Ask, "Which stores offer the best buys?"

In Your Community (Page 17)

Discuss ahead of time which items each person or group will compare so that there are as many different items as possible. Review the **U.S. to Metric Equivalents** chart on page 82 of this guide to make sure students understand U.S. units of measure. Create a chart for easy record keeping:

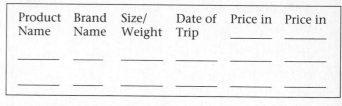

Product Name	Brand Name	Size/ Weight	Date of Trip	Price in ___	Price in ___

Total the savings with the class. Notice whether one store is cheaper than the other.

Figuring Out the U.S. (Page 18)

1. Have students bring in ads for things they would like to buy (bring in your own ads as a backup). Choose ads with lots of fine print and provide a balance of expensive and inexpensive items. Have students read the large print first, decide what the ad is offering, and then read the fine print. Ask, "Is the ad really offering what the large print says?" Talk about *restrictions, limitations,* and other key words, encouraging them to brainstorm definitions through contextual clues.

Your Turn (Page 18)

1. Ask questions such as: "What sorts of things are advertised in your native country? Where are they advertised? Do people pay attention to these ads?"

2. Make sure each student has an ad. First have students write what the ad seems to promise and then how the fine print limits the promise. Ask students to write about what this exercise teaches them about ads and other areas of their lives.

> Refer to page 34 of this guide for teaching suggestions for Review Unit One.

4 We Would Like a Phone

> **Competency**
> Interpreting information about obtaining a telephone
>
> **Content Reading**
> A telephone rate chart
>
> **Cultural Reading**
> Answering-machine messages
>
> **Structure**
> Present perfect
>
> **Listening/Speaking Tip**
> *ph-*, *-ght*, and *-tion*

Before You Listen (Page 21)

1. Introduce the illustration using the strategies on page 1 of this guide. Ask questions about the picture, such as: "Where do you think these people are? Why do you think people would come to this place? What do you think the reading will be about?" Ask students if they have telephones; if they do, ask whether they pay their bills in person or by mail. Ask, "What do you think *in person* means?" Have students ask each other questions based on the picture.

2. Teach key vocabulary such as *brand new*, *phone service*, and *bill*. Encourage students to ask about any vocabulary items that are indicated in the picture.

Dialogue (Page 22)

1. Present the dialogue orally, choosing from the strategies on page 1 of this guide.

2. After students have heard the dialogue twice, check comprehension with questions such as: "Is the phone for a business or a home? Do Nilda and Kim have a bank account? Can they use Nilda's uncle's phone?"

3. Students may read the dialogue aloud in groups of three, taking the roles of Kim, Nilda, and the service representative and then switching roles so that each student reads each part.

Talking It Over (Page 23)

1. After you have discussed the questions in the student text, have students talk about any experiences they've had getting telephones in their native countries. Encourage them to compare these experiences with what it is like to get a telephone in the United States.

2. Divide the class into two teams. Organize a debate, with one team talking about the value of having a telephone and the other team talking about the telephone as a problem or an unnecessary nuisance. Tell them the idea of a debate is to convince the other team that your position is right, even if they don't completely agree with what you're saying. The idea is for students to practice their speaking and listening skills and to learn to disagree in an appropriate manner.

Working Together (Page 23)

1. Role-play a conversation with a student, asking the kinds of questions that might be asked of a potential telephone customer. Teach expressions such as: "Would you repeat that please? I'm sorry, I don't understand. Could you speak more slowly please?"

2. Have students brainstorm possible completions for the dialogue while you write their ideas on the board. Pair students for practice and circulate, listening to the various conversations. Ask for volunteers to perform their conversation for the class.

Real Talk (Page 23)

1. This is a good time for a dictionary lesson. There are dictionaries available that have notes to the student. One good reference is the *Longman Dictionary of American English* (White Plains, N.Y.: Longman, Inc., 1983). For example, on pages with words beginning with *f*, the dictionary may explain that many words that begin with the "f" sound are spelled with *ph*. If you don't have access to such dictionaries, you might want to make copies of some sample words with each sound and have the students find other examples in the dictionary or even in this book.

Some samples are:
ph: photograph, philosophy, phobia,
   physical, sophomore
tion: constitution, election, conversation,
   communication

2. Have students make their own lists in pairs or groups and present them to the class. They might even try to guess what any unfamiliar words mean.

Putting It Together (Page 24)

1. Explain the present perfect tense as just another useful form of a verb. Ask different students where they lived before (past time), where they live now (present time), and how long they have lived at their new address (present perfect time, which shows the past continuing into the present). Write their responses on the board, underlining each verb and talking about what it tells them about time. Use the irregular verb list on page 84 of the student text to show past participles, explaining that regular past participles end in *-ed*. Some examples are *lived, watched,* and *signed.* Encourage them to ask and answer questions using the present perfect tense.

2. Ask questions using *since* and *for* to see if students can figure out the difference. Have them ask questions with *since* and *for* and write them on the board for other students to answer.

3. The exercise in the book can be done orally, used as a writing exercise, or both. When the exercise is completed, have several pairs read the conversation and be sure everyone understands important vocabulary.

Read and Think (Page 25)

1. Read the entire passage and ask students to put each paragraph in their own words to be sure they understand. Ask them which expression in the passage means *beat the rates* (*cut down the cost*). Go over the chart and discuss the questions together.

2. Talk about long-distance calls in the United States. Sometimes it's more expensive to call someone in another part of the same state than it is to call someone hundreds of miles away. Your local telephone company will supply you with free directories for your students.

In Your Community (Page 25)

1. Have a representative from your local telephone company come in and talk to your students about question 1 or assign pairs of students to get this information.

2. Using your local directories, answer question 2 together by listing local emergency numbers on the board. Be sure students make copies. Discuss the kinds of information they need to give when calling an emergency number. For example, they need to give their names, location of the emergency (including street and city), and the type of emergency. Stress the importance of speaking slowly and clearly. Have students role-play some emergency situations such as reporting a fire, a choking incident, or an automobile accident.

3. For question 3, encourage students to compare the cost of calling different countries. As they answer question 4, discussing the various long-distance companies, ask, "How did you learn about them? Which do you like best? Why?"

Figuring Out the U.S. (Page 26)

Have students work in pairs to create a message for their imaginary answering machines. Write some of their messages on the board. Then have students call each other, with Person A being the machine and Person B leaving a message.

Your Turn (Page 26)

Have students answer the questions as a class. Then divide them into two teams, with one team debating what's good and the other what's not so good about answering machines. Remind them about the purpose of debates, which is outlined in the **Talking It Over** section of this chapter.

5 But We Did Pay It!

Competency
Understanding telephone bills

Content Reading
A telephone bill

Cultural Reading
Telephone customs

Structure
Should/Shouldn't

Listening/Speaking Tip
Two sounds for *th*

Before You Listen (Page 27)

1. Introduce the illustration using the strategies on page 1 of this guide. Have students ask each other additional questions based on the picture.

2. Ask questions about the title, such as "What do you think this chapter will be about?" Encourage students to discuss what they see in the picture and relate it to their own feelings. Discuss the questions in the student text. Ask for a show of hands in response to question 3. Try to get an idea of what an average phone bill is for class members.

3. Teach key vocabulary such as *payment*, *owe*, *check*, *money order*, *on hold*, and *received*. Also encourage students to ask about any vocabulary items that are indicated in the picture.

Dialogue (Page 28)

1. Present the dialogue orally, choosing from the strategies on page 1 of this guide.

2. After students have heard the dialogue twice, check their comprehension with questions such as: "Did Kim and Nilda pay the new bill? Did Kim and Nilda pay by check or by money order?"

3. Students may read the dialogue aloud in groups of four, taking the roles of Kim, Nilda, Mrs. B., and the service and then switching roles so that each student reads each part.

Talking It Over (Page 29)

Discuss the questions in the student text and have groups prepare responses to share with the class concerning any personal experiences relating to questions 5, 6, and 7. Discuss ways to correct errors on telephone bills. Encourage students to write down the name of the person they spoke with at the telephone company and the date and time they tried to correct their bill.

Working Together (Page 29)

Role-play the practice conversation with a student, adding a question about where to mail your payment. Then have students role-play, asking and answering questions about the phone bill on page 28 of the student text. You might want to bring in a similar page from an old phone bill to discuss any local features they should know about. Use an overhead projector or make copies of the bill so students can role-play using any new information.

Real Talk (Page 29)

Read the paragraph to your students. Tell them to listen to the "th" sounds as they follow the reading in their books. You may want to read it more than once. For information about voiced and voiceless sounds, see page 14 of this guide. Ask students if they notice anything about the way the words are spelled and the way the "th" sound is pronounced. The "th" has a hard, or voiced, sound before a vowel (*a*, *e*, *i*, *o*, *u*, and *y*) and a soft, or voiceless, sound before a consonant. Have them find other "th" sounds either in the dictionary or in this unit.

Putting It Together (Page 30)

1. Sometimes *should* and *shouldn't* express an opinion about what is considered good or bad, polite or impolite. For example, "You *should* pay your phone bill on time" means it is honest and prudent to do so. However, "One *shouldn't* make noise when eating in the United States" means it's impolite to do this.

2. Model *Practice A* by writing one sentence together on the board. Then let students work individually or in pairs to complete the

---

practice. Ask for volunteers to put sentences on the board and discuss them.

3. *Practice B* can be done with students working in pairs, asking where Mrs. B. should put the phone and then saying why they think that's a good place. When all suggestions are completed, decide together which is really the best place. Remind them to respond to their partner's answers if they think a *shouldn't* sentence is more appropriate. For example, they may say, "She shouldn't put the phone on the counter next to the stove because that might be dangerous." Be sure they're writing down the new words in a notebook or using their texts to record important words that might come up, such as *dangerous*.

Read and Think (Page 31)

1. Refer to the pre-reading strategies on page 3 of this guide. It would be wise to suggest that students look over the questions before beginning to read.

2. Talk about the abbreviations and use a map to find the places referred to. Explain that day, night, and evening rates are based on the time zone of the caller. Talk about the fact that it is three hours earlier in California than it is in New Jersey, so that people in California who call New Jersey at the night rate (after 11 P.M.) will be reaching the number they're calling at 2 A.M.. Refer them to the **Continental U.S. Time Zones** map on page 81 of the student text.

3. Talk about area codes, asking students the telephone codes for their native countries. Have students read the bill and discuss the answers to anything that may puzzle them. Have them use telephone books (see **In Your Community**, which follows) to help solve any mysteries. Ask questions such as: "What do you think the FCC (Federal Communications Commission) Subscriber Line Charge is for? What does *itemized* mean?" Encourage students to bring in copies of their own telephone bills to discuss.

In Your Community (Page 31)

Give one telephone directory to each student (see page 17 under **Read and Think** in this guide). Have students turn to the Contents and discuss the components. As they answer the questions in this section, notice whether they need practice with alphabetical order and simple abbreviations. Offer help where appropriate.

Figuring Out the U.S. (Page 32)

As students read, have them compare the information in each paragraph with information about their native countries. Ask how people think about time in their native countries. Compare their answers with the information in the third paragraph of the reading. Discuss ways to deal with crank or obscene phone calls and introduce any other information that is relevant to your community.

Your Turn (Page 32)

Have students make a chart comparing the United States and their native countries, using questions 1, 2, 3, and 6.

6 It's Fun to Eat Out

Before You Listen (Page 33)

1. Introduce the illustration using the strategies on page 1 of this guide. Ask, "Do you agree with the title?" Have students discuss the picture, comparing what they see with local fast-food restaurants. List on the board some of the responses they give for questions 3 and 5 in the student text. Have students ask each other additional questions based on the picture.

2. Teach key vocabulary such as *fast food*, *menu*, *change*, and *tax*. Encourage students to ask about any vocabulary items that are indicated in the picture.

Dialogue (Page 34)

1. Present the dialogue orally, choosing from the strategies on page 1 of this guide. Ask about Lee's response to Naresh's question. Ask, "Why did Lee answer this way?" Point out that Lee probably didn't have a strong opinion about the quality of food at the restaurant.

2. After students have heard the dialogue twice, check their comprehension with questions such as: "Is Lee hungry? Does Lee take cream in his coffee? Does Naresh want dressing on his salad?"

3. Students may read the dialogue aloud in groups of three, taking the roles of Naresh,

Lee, and the cashier and then switching roles so that each student reads each part.

Talking It Over (Page 35)

After students discuss the questions, talk as a group about question 2 in the student text. Write on the board their suggestions for appropriate ways to dispute a bill. Have them role-play the situation using the suggestions on the board. Ask students if they go to restaurants. If they do, ask about the kinds of restaurants they like and why they like them. Ask questions such as: "What local restaurants can you tell us about? Do you like them? Do you have to make reservations? What do you think it means to *make reservations*?"

Working Together (Page 35)

To remind students of their suggestions about how to dispute a bill in **Talking It Over**, have students role-play the situations with Naresh and Lee. Ask for volunteers to create another similar situation to present to the class. Talk about attitude and tone of voice. You might want to introduce this by saying the same phrase (for example, "Would you like your change?") in both a helpfully pleasant tone of voice and in an obnoxiously sarcastic tone of voice.

Real Talk (Page 35)

List other polite expressions—such as "I beg your pardon"—on the board for students to practice in conversations. Have groups of three role-play a conversation in which one of them interrupts. Record on the board the part of the conversation that begins with the interruption. Ask what some responses might be. For example: "Yes?" "Just a minute," or "What's the matter?" While the class is working, say "Excuse me" and see what the reaction is.

Putting It Together (Page 36)

1. Illustrate each example of a superlative using items and people in the room. Ask questions such as: "Who is the tallest person in this class? What is the funniest thing that has happened to you in this class? What is the

least expensive restaurant in this
neighborhood?"

2. Introduce this as a writing exercise with
   students comparing their answers in pairs.

Read and Think (Page 37)

1. Go over the menu, making sure students
   understand everything. Ask students to
   compare the food on this menu with the
   foods in their native countries. Bring in some
   menus from local restaurants (including
   ethnic ones) for comparison.

2. Put some of the responses to question 3 on
   the board for comparison and discussion. Ask
   questions such as: "Do you usually eat out or
   do you usually eat at home? Why? Which
   will you do in the future? Why?"

In Your Community (Page 37)

Before students make their trip, create a chart
together. Use this chart as a model:

Food	Size	Cholesterol	Contents	Fat	Sodium
___	___	___	___	___	___
___	___	___	___	___	___

According to law, nutritional information must
be available by law in fast-food restaurants and
frozen yogurt and ice cream stores. You can have
students make a master chart together using
their information and either make copies for
each of them or set it up on the board for them
to copy.

Figuring Out the U.S. (Page 38)

Discuss the reading paragraph by paragraph.
After you've discussed questions 1 through 5 in
Your Turn, ask questions such as: "How do you
get a waiter's or waitress's attention in your
native country? Do people leave tips in your
native country? If so, how? Do tips have to do
with the price on the bill? Is tax added to
restaurant bills in your native country? Do
people take home 'doggie bags'?"

Your Turn (Page 38)

Create an experience chart on the board based
on a few students' responses to question 6. Then
pair or group students and have them create
their own experience chart to share with the rest
of the class.

The chart could be structured as follows:

Restaurant Experience Chart		
	U.S. Restaurants	_____ Restaurants
Prices	High	
Quantity of Food		
Quality of Food		
Service		

**Refer to page 34 of this guide for teaching
suggestions for Review Unit Two.**

7 It's a Luxury We Can't Afford

Competency
Interpreting information about personal and family budgets

Content Reading
A credit card statement

Cultural Reading
Budgeting

Structure
Would like

Listening/Speaking Tip
Can/Can't

Before You Listen (Page 41)

1. Introduce the illustration using the strategies on page 1 of this guide.

2. Teach key vocabulary such as: *luxury, necessity, budget, bargain,* and *afford*. Ask, "What do you think the luxury in the title is?" Encourage students to talk about what things are luxuries and necessities for them. Ask if those things have changed since they came to the United States, and if so, how.

Dialogue (Page 42)

1. Present the dialogue orally, choosing from the strategies on page 1 of this guide.

2. After students have heard the dialogue twice, talk about a *sales pitch* and how the salesman is trying to sell the giant-screen TV. Ask students how they would react to this kind of sales pitch.

3. Students may read the dialogue aloud in groups of three, taking the roles of the salesman, Dipti, and Naresh and then switching roles so that each student reads each part.

Talking It Over (Page 43)

1. Make two lists on the board—one for necessities and one for luxuries, as suggested in question 5. Talk about the fact that what's a luxury to one person may be a necessity to

another. Create a monthly budget together using figures students think are appropriate. Be sure they include more than rent, food, and phone bills.

2. Brainstorm with the class about the differences among paying for items with cash, paying with a credit card, and paying on an installment plan. Suggest several items (a car, a television, and a coat, for example) and ask individuals how they would pay for each item if they were buying it.

3. Divide the class into three groups, with one group making a chart of the pros and cons of paying in cash, the second group focusing on using a credit card, and the third group dealing with making monthly payments. Have each group present its chart for class discussion and comparison.

Working Together (Page 43)

1. Write the sample conversation on the board and have students complete it. Ask volunteers to present the dialogue to the class; then discuss different ways to deal with this type of situation. The laws vary about who is responsible for an item a child breaks in a store, so encourage students to contact their attorney general's office.

2. Assign some pairs to role-play a scene in which a salesperson is pushing a certain product and a customer is "just looking" or not sure of what he/she wants. Discuss together appropriate ways to deal with this kind of situation. Outside the classroom, students may be on either side of the counter.

Real Talk (Page 43)

1. Read the sentences naturally, so that *can* does indeed sound like "kin" and *can't* is stressed, the final *t* assimilating to the sound after it.

2. Write these sentences on the board for students to practice together:

Partner A: Can you go shopping with me?
Partner B: I can't get a baby-sitter, and I can't go shopping with the baby.

Partner A: I can go shopping for you if you can't come with me.

Partner B: Thanks. I hope I can do a favor for you someday.

Refer to the strategies on page 1 of this guide for methods of presenting a dialogue.

Putting It Together (Page 44)

1. Review contractions, asking what letters the apostrophe could replace in *we'd*. Write the contractions *I'd, you'd, he'd, she'd, we'd,* and *they'd* on the board and ask students to write the words each contraction represents. Have them use some of these contractions in sentences.

2. Begin *Practice A* as a pair discussion and then extend it to a class discussion.

3. Do the first sentence from *Practice B* as a class. Have students complete the written portion individually and then have them work with a partner to compare their responses. Have students report on their partners' responses to the class so they get practice speaking in the third-person singular.

Read and Think (Page 45)

1. Introduce the important vocabulary on the credit card statement. For other reading strategies, refer to page 3 of this guide.

2. After discussing questions 1–3, do question 4 together, figuring out the cost of the TV, the number of payments they'd have to make, and how much interest they'd have to pay per month based on a 19.4 percent annual percentage rate. (They would have to make 14 payments and pay $63.71 in interest.)

3. Talk about the responsibilities involved in using a credit card, addressing questions 5 and 6 in the student text in particular. Ask why they think billing disputes should be put in writing. Talk about keeping a copy of any correspondence one sends to a credit card company as proof that directions have been followed. You might want to write a model letter as a class to the ACE Credit Card Company, disputing a charge on the bill.

In Your Community (Page 45)

Have students bring in credit card applications from local banks or stores. Bring in some applications yourself, in case some students forget. Talk about any new vocabulary or concepts. Have students go over applications together and fill them out. Discuss credit cards that charge an annual fee. When you discuss interest payments, explain to them that what looks like very little (1-1/2 percent per month) can really be a great deal (18 percent per year.)

Figuring Out the U.S. (Page 46)

1. Discuss the expressions "over their heads" and "keeping up with the Joneses." Ask questions such as: "Do people get into debt in your native country? If so, how do they talk about it (do they use expressions such as 'over their heads')? Are people in your native country divided into economic classes? What are they?" Refer to the reading strategies on page 3 of this guide.

2. Ask students to think very seriously about the next question and to be very honest with themselves: "Are you affected by commercials? If so, what kind?" Follow up with questions such as: "When you see a food commercial, do you get something to eat?" Explain that some people are tempted to eat; some to drink; others to buy. Ask students if they fit into any of these categories. If they decide that they are influenced by commercials, ask what they think they can do about it. Ask whether they are tempted to buy things that would not be within their budgets.

Your Turn (Page 46)

Have students work in groups to make lists of what is good and what is bad about credit cards. Put the headings *Good* and *Bad* on the board and have each group read one of its statements. Write that statement on the board under the appropriate column. Ask students whether they think credit cards have more good features than bad features. Brainstorm with them about how to control the bad features.

8 How Do We Get There?

Before You Listen (Page 47)

1. Introduce the illustration using strategies on page 1 of this guide. Ask questions about the picture, having students describe it in as much detail as possible. Introduce necessary vocabulary, such as *department*, *directory*, *electrical appliances*, *cookware*, *housewares*, *escalator*, and *toasters*.

2. If possible, bring in a toaster or another small appliance and discuss how to use it and what one might look for when shopping for it.

Dialogue (Page 48)

1. Present the dialogue orally, choosing from the strategies on page 1 of this guide.

2. Ask students about large department stores or shopping malls they may have visited. After students have heard the dialogue twice, check their comprehension with questions such as, "What department are toasters in?"

3. Students may read the dialogue aloud in groups of four, taking the roles of Kim, Nilda, Mrs. B., and the clerk and then switching roles so that each student reads each part.

Talking It Over (Page 49)

1. Have students make a list of other items that might be found in the Housewares Department.

2. Ask questions such as: "Was Mrs. B's idea of looking for toasters with the electrical appliances good or bad? Why?"

3. Have students compare their early shopping experiences in the United States. Ask questions such as: "Did you have any difficulties? Could you understand store directories? What about spoken directions? Did you understand sizes and electrical currents? Is it easier to shop now?"

4. Make a chart together of basic differences between shopping in department stores in the United States and shopping in students' native countries. Have students tell which they prefer and why.

	In the U.S.	In _____
Prices		
Variety		
Quality		
Difficulty		

Working Together (Page 49)

Make a list together on the board of items students can buy in a department store. Make another list of directional words such as: *to the left*, *to the right*, *north*, *south*, *east* and *west*. You might want to get the directory from a local department store or make a floor plan for a discount store in your community and have students practice asking for and giving directions. Then have groups make their own smaller directories, and based on them, answer each other's questions about where to go for specific items.

Real Talk (Page 49)

Explain that students will hear very few "g" sounds when people speak but that the letter *g* is always written in words that end in *-ing*. Have some students use the words to create sentences on the board and have other students read the sentences aloud. Make sure they see and hear the difference.

Putting It Together (Page 50)

1. Embedded questions are really questions turned into statements. Write some embedded questions on the board and show how the subject and verb look the same in an embedded question as they do in any sentence. In a question, the verb comes first; in a statement, the subject comes first.

   Where are they?
   I wonder where they are.

   Next, explain that questions that take *do* leave the *do* out of embedded questions:

   How does this toaster work?
   I wonder how this toaster works.

   Be sure to include present tense embedded questions with third-person singular pronouns, such as:

   How much does it cost?
   I wonder how much it costs.

2. Do the first sentence of *Practice A* together and have students copy it. When they complete the rest of the exercise, have some volunteers read their answers aloud and have others put their answers on the board for discussion.

3. Have students work on *Practice B* in pairs and encourage them to try some questions with *do* and with the third-person singular, such as: "Does Anna know when Sox Galore opens?"

Read and Think (Page 51)

1. Tell students about a garage sale (tag sale, yard sale) that you have been to. Describe what was for sale, who was selling it, and what you bought and why. Talk about the fact that items at garage sales are bought and sold "as is." Explain that the person conducting the garage sale may or may not permit you to test an item to see if it works (plug in a radio, for example) but that it doesn't hurt to ask.

2. Review directional terms (*to the left, to the right,* and so on). After students have

answered the questions in the student text, have them look at the map and ask each other how to get from one place to another. Lead with questions such as, "How do I get to Discount Appliances from the school?"

3. Ask, "Is there anything like a garage sale in your native country?" If they go to garage sales in the U.S., ask questions such as: "How do you usually find out about garage sales? How do you get directions to garage sales?"

In Your Community (Page 51)

1. Tell students to take note of the stores they pass when they come to school or go to work. Make a list together of the different kinds of stores in the community. Ask questions such as: "Are these stores easy to get to? Do you need a car to get to them? Can you use public transportation? How do you get to the local mall or shopping center?" Ask volunteers to pick out local stores and explain how to get there on public transportation, in a car, or by walking.

2. Have each student draw a simple map showing how to get from the school to a favorite store. Have students work from their maps and explain to a partner exactly how to get there. Then have the partner repeat the directions to be sure they were clear.

Figuring Out the U.S. (Page 52)

Have students read the entire passage first and then go over the reading paragraph by paragraph. Ask questions such as: "Have you been to a mall? What do you think window-shopping means? If you drive to the mall, do you ever have trouble finding your car? Have you ever lost the person you went to the mall with? If so, what did you do? How did you feel?"

Your Turn (Page 52)

Have students make a chart of the pros and cons of malls using much of the information expressed above. Discuss whether there are more good or bad features to shopping at malls.

9 May I Help You?

Before You Listen (Page 53)

1. Introduce the illustration using the strategies on page 1. As students talk about the picture and answer the questions, encourage them to be specific about why they like or don't like to shop for clothes in department stores. Ask questions such as: "Is it hard to find a salesperson? Are there too many choices? Is it confusing?"

2. Teach key vocabulary, such as *return*, *exchange*, *receipt*, and *refund*.

3. If anyone has ever returned an item, have him or her tell about the experience. Ask questions such as, "Where is it easier to return an item: in a department store or a small store? Why do you think that is?" Share some of your experiences with the class.

Dialogue (Page 54)

1. Present the dialogue orally, choosing from the strategies on page 1 of this guide.

2. After students have heard the dialogue twice, check their comprehension with questions such as, "Did Nilda exchange the blouse?"

3. Students may read the dialogue aloud in pairs, taking the roles of Nilda and the saleswoman and then switching roles so that each student reads each part.

Talking It Over (Page 55)

1. After the students talk about questions 1, 2, and 3, discuss the policies in stores where students shop. Ask questions such as: "Do you know what the return policy is in that store (exchange only, complete refund, or no refunds or exchanges)? How does this affect the way you shop in this store? Do you shop in a store with a no-return policy? Why?" (Many discount stores have no-return policies, but the savings are worth careful shopping.)

2. Point out that each store has its own return/credit policy.

3. With question 6, ask students what Nilda should get if she exchanges her blouse for a less expensive one (perhaps a credit she can use in the store). Talk about saving receipts and credit statements.

Working Together (Page 55)

Talk about the importance of having a positive attitude when returning or exchanging an item. A polite but firm approach is usually better than a hostile one, since the salesperson making the exchange is an innocent party. Complete the conversation together on the board, have students practice it, and ask volunteers to present it to the class. Then have students try an impromptu dialogue, exchanging whatever items they'd like. Discuss afterward which approaches seemed most effective and why.

Real Talk (Page 55)

This is another reduction students must get used to hearing without letting it affect their spelling. Read the sentences aloud and ask volunteers to create some *let me* sentences on the board and have other volunteers read them so they can hear the difference between the spoken and written words.

Putting It Together (Page 56)

1. Say, "If you are hungry now, raise your hand." Students should raise their hands only if they are hungry. Write the sentence on the board. Have students use the example in the grammar box as a model to rephrase the sentence above.

2. Do sentence 1 of *Practice A* together and have students finish the exercise individually. Have students put some sentences on the board and have others read the sentences to the class. See who can switch their sentences around so that they can be read either way.

3. Walk around the room as students work on *Practice B*, helping only those who have real problems. Again, have students put some of their work on the board and have others read their sentences to the class. As another example, say to students, "If you all understand, then we can go on to the next part of the lesson."

Read and Think (Page 57)

1. Bring in several items of clothing with readable labels on them. Try to bring in examples of written instructions and care symbols. Have a volunteer write the information from the labels on the board. Discuss why labels provide such information.

2. Make a list together of kinds of information included on clothing labels in the United States. Go over the vocabulary and symbols on the labels. Make sure students understand washing and drying instructions. Ask, "Have you ever shrunk or faded an item of clothing because you didn't follow the instructions?"

3. Ask questions such as: "How much of the information on the labels is helpful to you? Why? What information, if any, do you think is unimportant? Why?"

In Your Community (Page 57)

Tell students to look inside their clothing at home, either at the neckline or in one of the seams, and write the information on the chart in the student text. Have them bring in their charts and together make a class chart from their information. You might want to include some of your clothing labels in this chart, too.

Figuring Out the U.S. (Page 58)

Ask students about trips they have made to department stores or malls. Ask specifically about their experiences with salesclerks. Refer to the reading strategies on page 3 in this guide.

Your Turn (Page 58)

1. Discuss the frustrations sometimes involved in finding a salesclerk in a department store or, conversely, having a salesclerk follow you around when you're just looking. How does this compare with shopping in their native countries?

2. If you have a personal experience to relate about question 5, share it with the class, especially if you're one of those people who find it hard to say no to a salesclerk who has spent a lot of time with you. Together, develop some strategies for dealing with similar situations.

3. As a writing exercise, have students work in pairs to develop a dialogue based on the strategies you have worked out above. Ask volunteers to present their dialogues to the class.

> Refer to page 34 of this guide for teaching suggestions for Review Unit Three.

10 I'm Busy Right Now

Before You Listen (Page 61)

1. Introduce the illustration using the strategies on page 1 of this guide. As students describe what they see in the picture, ask them if the scene looks at all familiar to them. Ask questions such as: "Do you ever get annoying phone calls when you're trying to do something important? If so, how do you handle them?"

2. Teach key vocabulary, such as *go wrong with*, *warranty*, *appliance*, *replace*, and *service agreement*. Point out the potential disasters in the illustration.

Dialogue (Page 62)

1. Present the dialogue orally, choosing from the strategies on page 1 of this guide.

2. After students have heard the dialogue twice, check their comprehension with questions such as, "Did Dipti buy the service agreement?"

3. Students may read the dialogue aloud in pairs, taking the roles of Dipti and the salesman and then switching roles so that each student reads each part.

Talking It Over (Page 63)

1. Talk about high-pressure salespeople and how to deal with them.

2. In answering questions 3 and 4, discuss reading the fine print on agreements before purchasing them. Have students share any experiences they have had with purchasing service agreements. Ask such questions as: "What item was the agreement for? Did you ever have to use the service agreement? Did you save money by having the service agreement or would it have been cheaper without it?"

Working Together (Page 63)

After partners practice the conversation they have developed, have several pairs present their dialogue to the class. Afterward, talk about how different salespeople tried to sell the *Willow News* and the various ways customers responded. Ask which ways of selling were most effective and why.

Real Talk (Page 63)

1. Put the following sentence on the board for students to see and to listen to as you read it with natural reduced sounds: *Reading a warranty is better than hearing about it.*

2. If you haven't already done so, this is a good time to introduce ordinal numbers in the context of the "th" sound. Write *first* through *twentieth* on the board and have students repeat the words. Have students return to the dialogue on page 62 of the student text and practice the "through the nineteenth" lines in pairs, substituting different ordinal numbers. Remind them that dates are written in Arabic numbers but are read and pronounced as ordinal numbers.

Putting It Together (Page 64)

1. This exercise shows some of the subtle differences involved in speaking American English. The small difference between *could* (are you able to) and *would* (a slightly firmer request) can be noted if it doesn't confuse students. The words are really used interchangeably today. The same is true of *can* and *will*, with *can* noting ability, and *will* expressing a promise.

2. Do the first sentence of *Practice A* together. Insert the word *please* to reinforce the polite request. When the exercise is completed, have different students read what they have written and encourage other students to respond.

3. *Practice B* should provide a variety of conversations to be presented to the class. Have them work as a group first to compose a sample dialogue.

Read and Think (Page 65)

1. Before students read the warranty, have them read the subheads and try to predict what each portion of the document is about. For other reading strategies, refer to page 3 of this guide.

2. Encourage students to ask questions about the warranty if there is anything unclear to them after they answer the questions. Ask the meanings of words such as *specific*, *legal*, *defects*, and *negligence*. If students use dictionaries, be sure they choose the definition that most closely corresponds with the meanings here. Encourage them to use their new-found definitions to reword the parts of the warranty they're not sure of.

3. Have students work in groups to reword the warranty so they can explain it to someone who speaks less English than they do.

In Your Community (Page 65)

Bring in a warranty and chart the information on the board using the example in the student text. Have students read from their own warranties or make copies of your warranty and have them furnish the information necessary to complete the chart. Ask questions such as: "How good is your warranty? What types of items have the best warranties? Does a warranty affect your buying habits? If so, how?"

Figuring Out the U.S. (Page 66)

Talk about the different ways to buy things cheaply in the United States. Relate the conversation to your community, emphasizing garage or yard sales, discount stores, thrift stores, outlet stores, and so on.

Your Turn (Page 66)

1. Relate some of your own experiences if you have ever shopped in any of the places mentioned in the **Figuring Out the U.S.** section. Encourage students to relate their experiences in answering questions 2 and 3.

2. Have students tell not only where used items are bought but also what kinds of items are bought used in their native countries. Ask them how this compares with the United States. Ask questions such as: "Can you get items with warranties in your native country? If so, where? What kinds of items are they?"

3. As a writing exercise, students could respond to question 2 or 3 with a personal experience. You might want to create an experience chart first so they have a writing model (see page 21 of this guide).

4. Have students work in pairs to write a dialogue or a short play based on an experience one of the students has had with either paying too much money for something or saving a lot of money on a purchase.

11 I Want to Think It Over

Competency
Interpreting information related to the selection and purchase of a car

Content Reading
Car ads

Cultural Reading
Driving in the U.S.

Structure
Wh-questions

Listening/Speaking Tip
And/" 'n' "

Before You Listen (Page 67)

1. Introduce the illustration using the strategies on page 1. Ask students if they know the various vehicle types in the illustration (two-door hatchback, van, pickup truck, station wagon).

2. Teach other key vocabulary, such as *model*, *trade in*, *dealer*, *car lot*, and *automatic transmission* (as opposed to *standard transmission*). Have them talk about the picture and relate it to any experiences they have had buying something expensive.

Dialogue (Page 68)

1. Present the dialogue orally, choosing from the strategies on page 1 of this guide.

2. After students have heard the dialogue twice, check their comprehension with questions such as, "Did Lee buy a used car or a new car?"

3. Students may read the dialogue aloud in groups of three, taking the roles of Lee, the salesman, and Naresh, and then switching roles so that each student reads each part.

Talking It Over (Page 69)

1. If you have bought a car recently, share your experiences. Have students share similar experiences they may have had.

2. As you discuss question 1, make a list of the features offered with the new car.

3. Have students work on question 3 individually and then share their answers with the class. Ask why they listed things in the order they did, and find out what kinds of questions they would ask if they were looking to buy a car.

Working Together (Page 69)

After students complete their conversations, have several volunteers perform theirs for the class. Ask questions such as: "Who was the most convincing salesperson? Why? Who was the most careful shopper? Why? What strategies for wise car shopping have you learned?" Write their strategies on the board.

Real Talk (Page 69)

By now, students are familiar with the fact that many words are spelled one way and pronounced another, as speakers leave out letters and slide one word into another. After repeating the example for them, have students write some sentences with *and* and choose several of the sentences to be written on the board for other students to read. You may also want pairs to exchange sentences and read them to each other. Encourage them to talk about the differences. It's important that students understand what they're hearing when it is different from the written form of the word.

Putting It Together (Page 70)

1. Review the meanings of the five wh- and *how* words, reminding students that *who* refers only to people. Ask students questions about themselves such as: "Who has a car? When did you buy it? Where?"

2. When students complete *Practice A*, have them read their questions to the class.

3. Make a list on the board from the responses in *Practice B*. Then have students put the questions in order of importance using words like *first*, *next*, and *then*.

Read and Think (Page 71)

Abbreviations in classified ads are extremely difficult for non-English speakers and many native speakers, too. Go over each ad in the student text together to figure out what the abbreviations stand for. You might want to make a matching game on the board: write the words on one side and their abbreviations on the other in random order, and have students draw lines from the words to their correct abbreviations.

In Your Community (Page 71)

1. Bring in classified ads from your local newspaper and have students do the same. Have them make a list of abbreviations and try to guess their meanings from contextual clues.

2. Have groups create a game with their abbreviations—a crossword puzzle, a matching game, or a sentence-completion game, for example.

3. If the Better Business Bureau's Auto Line (a recorded information service) is available in your community, have students call it. You may also wish to invite an expert on consumer fraud to speak to the class about buying new or used cars.

Figuring Out the U.S. (Page 72)

1. Discuss the terms *rural* and *urban*. Ask what areas students live in or have lived in. Ask questions such as: "Are cars a necessity where you live? Why or why not?"

2. Ask questions such as: "How many of you have driver's licenses? Was a license difficult to get? What did you have to do? Did you take your driver's test in English?" (In some states, the written test is offered in a number of languages.)

3. Talk about car insurance and the difference in rates depending on age, sex, and where you live. You might want to bring someone in to talk about car insurance in your state, especially if your state has very high or very low rates, no-fault insurance, obligatory insurance, or other unusual features.

Your Turn (Page 72)

1. If there is a local SADD (Students Against Drunk Driving) or MADD (Mothers Against Drunk Driving) group, invite a speaker to talk to the class about the destructive results of driving while under the influence of drugs or alcohol. Ask questions such as: "Is drunk driving a problem in your native countries? If it is, what happens to someone who is arrested for drunk driving?" Discuss the penalties in your community.

2. In answer to question 4, talk about the price of cars in relation to people's incomes. What sounds like not much money for a car in one country can be a year's salary for some people.

12 That Makes Sense

Before You Listen (Page 73)

1. Introduce the illustration using the strategies
on page 1. Have students discuss the picture
in detail, making sure they understand the
words they see. Ask questions such as: "Why
do you think Kim and Nilda are sitting at a
desk rather than standing in line? What are
the people in line waiting for?"

2. Teach key vocabulary, such as *bank*, *bank
statement*, *deposit*, *withdrawal*, *teller*, and
checking account.

Dialogue (Page 74)

1. Present the dialogue orally, choosing from
the strategies on page 1 of this guide.

2. After students have heard the dialogue twice,
check comprehension with questions such as:
"Why are Nilda and Kim at the bank?"

3. Students may read the dialogue aloud in
groups of three, taking the roles of the bank
officer, Kim, and Nilda and then switching
roles so that each student reads each part.

Talking It Over (Page 75)

Talk together about the importance of bank
statements and canceled checks and about
keeping them in a safe place for a period of time.
Be sure students understand why one would
keep canceled checks.

Working Together (Page 75)

1. Go over the deposit slip together, making
sure students understand the vocabulary and
what to do.

2. Bring in some deposit and withdrawal slips
from a local bank and have students work
with them in pairs. Have them create
fictitious names and account numbers or use
their own names. Have them fill out the slips
as they wish and hand them to their partners,
who will play the roles of bank tellers. The
students, playing bank tellers will say
something like: "I see you want to withdraw
$1,500, Mr. Rinzler. Is that correct?"

Real Talk (Page 75)

1. Tell the students that when a word ends in
-*ed*, it is pronounced in one of three possible
ways. Refer to the **Real Talk** section on page
14 of this guide for strategies on how to work
with voiced and voiceless sounds.

2. Write the words *subtract* and *decide* on the
board, one under the other. Underline the
final *t* in *subtract* and the final *d* in *decide* and
tell them that when words end with a "t" or
"d" sound, you hear an extra syllable when
you add -*ed* to them. Write -*ed* next to
subtract and -*d* next to *decide* and pronounce
them for the students. Under these, forming a
column, write the words *deposit*, *wait*, and
need. Have students pronounce the words,
then add -*ed* to them. Have students
pronounce them again, reminding them of
the rule. Write -*ed* at the top of the column to
show that the column is made up of words
that have an extra syllable when the -*ed*
ending is added.

3. Write the word *cancel* to the right of *subtract*.
Underline the *l* in *cancel* and write -*ed* next to
it. Have students put their fingers on their
vocal cords (refer to the **Real Talk** section on
page 14 of this guide) and say the word. The
final sound is voiced so they should feel their
voice boxes vibrate. When a word ends in a
voiced sound, the -*ed* is voiced and sounds
like "d." Put a *d* at the top of the column to

show that the column is made up of words that have the "d" sound when *-ed* is applied.

4. Follow the same procedure for *cash*, writing *t* at the top of the column to show that the voiceless word endings make *-ed* sound like "t."

The chart should now have three headings and look like this:

ed	*d*	*t*
subtracted	canceled	cashed
decided		
deposited		
waited		
needed		

5. Put the following words on the board: *endorse*, *explain*, *receive*, and *prove*. Have students say the words, add the *-ed* endings, say them again, and place them in the appropriate column.

Putting It Together (Page 76)

1. Review ordinal numbers. Talk about phrases of time coming at the beginning or end of a sentence. If you want to get involved with punctuation, tell them that when a time phrase comes at the beginning of a sentence, it is separated from the rest of the sentence by a comma.

2. Depending on your students, you might want to complete *Practice A* before discussing the time words to see how much they know.

3. *Practice B* can be shared with the class to create a series of short paragraphs.

Read and Think (Page 77)

1. Go over the check, making sure everyone understands the vocabulary and why the amount appears in numbers and in writing.

2. Go over the checkbook together, making sure students understand what the 101 and 102 refer to and why it's important to write the check number in the checkbook. Ask, "What do you think the word *transaction* means? Do you see any word you recognize in it?" They may be able to guess the meaning if they see *action* within the word.

In Your Community (Page 77)

Have students share their information with the class. Try to get information from more than one bank when feasible. Invite a speaker from a local bank to come in and talk with students about the bank's services and respond to their questions.

Figuring Out the U.S. (Page 78)

After the initial reading, go over the passage paragraph by paragraph, making sure students understand the vocabulary. Discuss automatic teller machines in your area, making sure students know that if they use them, they should exercise care with their cards, their codes, and where and when they withdraw money. Have them share any experiences or problems they've had with ATMs.

Your Turn (Page 78)

1. If ATM cards are common in their native countries, ask students to compare ATM cards there and in the U.S. If they are not common, ask how people "bank" in the students' native countries.

2. In response to question 4, have students make a list of the good and bad features of ATM cards.

3. You may wish to have students write a letter to a fictitious bank—First National Bank of Willow perhaps—to clear up an error that was made on some checks they ordered (perhaps someone's name was misspelled).

> Refer to page 34 of this guide for teaching suggestions for Review Unit 4.

Review Unit Teaching Suggestions

The purpose of the review units is to help students develop their communicative competence while reviewing the specific vocabulary and competencies presented in the student text. Each review unit is in the form of a two-page information-gap exercise. Students work in pairs and obtain information orally from their partners in order to complete their task.

To introduce the information-gap exercise, first divide the class into groups A and B. Then match each "Person A" with a "Person B" so that all students are working in pairs. Person A looks only at the first page of the information-gap exercise, while Person B looks only at the second page.

Review Unit One (Pages 19 and 20)

Review Unit One takes students back to some of the food ads they saw in Chapter 3 and gives them a chance to comparison shop with a partner. Using some new vocabulary along with the vocabulary introduced in Chapters 2 and 3, this exercise encourages students to compare the prices at both stores and determine which store has the best buys. Students can review contractions ("It's $1.29") and comparisons ("Orange juice is cheaper at Penny-Wise than at Bargain Market") as they discuss the stores.

Review Unit Two (Pages 39 and 40)

This crossword puzzle features vocabulary from Chapters 4–6. Students may refer to the Index on pages 85–86 for help. In this case Person A and Person B have the same puzzle, but Person A's has the words filled in going across and Person B's has the words filled in going down. Only by working together can the students complete the puzzle.

Review Unit Three (Pages 59 and 60)

Be sure students understand that each of them has a partially completed map of a mall. Their task is to talk with their partner to find the stores on their list and write the names of the stores in the appropriate places. Before students begin, elicit helpful vocabulary, such as *first level*, *second level*, *above*, *below*, *to the right*, *to the left*, *next to*, and so on.

Review Unit Four (Pages 79 and 80)

The final review unit highlights items from Chapters 10–12, such as a check and checkbook, a warranty, and a car ad. Students must ask each other questions about the items they have until they determine whether the items are the same or different. Encourage students to discuss the differences and what they mean. For example, Person A's warranty may be enforced only by the original purchaser, but Person B's warranty may be enforced by any purchaser. Ask questions such as: "Which warranty would you like to have? Why?"

IN GOOD HEALTH

ELIZABETH CLAIRE

Scope and Sequence

CHAPTER	COMPETENCIES	
Chapter 1 I Was Sick, but I'm Fine Now	• Describing general states of health • Inquiring about another person's health	• Responding politely to statements about health • Describing personal health habits
Chapter 2 What Can You Recommend?	• Asking for recommendations for over-the-counter preparations or home remedies • Understanding dosages and precautions on medicine labels	• Giving health-care advice for minor ailments
Chapter 3 Have You Been to Our Office?	• Making an appointment by telephone • Finding a doctor	• Asking for repetition of phone numbers • Filling out a health history form
Chapter 4 Show Me Where the Pain Is	• Understanding and responding to a doctor's questions • Describing symptoms	• Asking questions about proposed treatments
Chapter 5 We'll Have to Run Some Tests	• Asking questions to ensure accurate understanding of advice • Getting a prescription filled • Understanding labels on prescription medicine	• Reading instructions for medical tests
Chapter 6 Look at This Bill!	• Asking questions about insurance coverage • Filing a claim	• Applying for health insurance • Understanding a health insurance policy
Chapter 7 We Can't Pay the Doctor's Bills	• Inquiring about government health-assistance programs • Identifying local agencies that provide aid	• Requesting information by phone
Chapter 8 This Is an Emergency!	• Summoning help over the telephone	• Describing an accident
Chapter 9 Which Tooth Is Bothering You?	• Asking questions about dental care and treatment	• Inquiring about the cost of dental work
Chapter 10 Do You Worry Much?	• Describing emotional states	• Finding mental-health professionals
Chapter 11 That's Why It's Called Labor	• Asking for and understanding prenatal-care advice	• Identifying prenatal-care practices
Chapter 12 What's for Supper?	• Responding to questions about a balanced diet	• Identifying the four food groups • Describing and assessing one's diet

CONTENT READING	CULTURAL READING	STRUCTURE
Facts about the common cold	The American preoccupation with health	Present tense: questions and short answers
Medicine labels	Natural remedies for minor ailments	Commands
A health form	Comparing private doctors and clinics	Wh-questions: *when*
Symptoms of common health problems	Involvement in health care	Irregular past-tense verbs
Prescriptions and labels on prescription medicine	Alternative health care practitioners	Future with *going to*
A group health insurance policy	A health insurance application form	Future with *will*
Medicaid and Medicare	Bureaucracies and red tape	Verbs that take gerunds/Verbs that take infinitives
Emergency-room procedures	Deciding when emergency-room care is necessary	Past-continuous tense
Dental care	Painless dental techniques	*Should*
Types of professional and self-help groups	Seeking help for emotional difficulties	Frequency words
Tests during pregnancy	Birthing rooms and midwives	Comparative forms
Checking ingredients on food labels	Dieting in the United States	*Many/Much*

1 I Was Sick, but I'm Fine Now

> **Competency**
> Describing general states of health
>
> **Content Reading**
> Facts about the common cold
>
> **Cultural Reading**
> The American preoccupation with health
>
> **Structures**
> Present tense: questions and short answers
>
> **Listening/Speaking Tip**
> Two sounds of the letter *s*

Before You Listen (Page 1)

1. Introduce the illustration using the strategies on page 1 of this guide. Have students ask each other additional questions based on the picture.

2. Teach key vocabulary such as *a cold*, *a fever*, *ill*, *making (him) sick*, *feel better*, and *worry*. Clarify meanings without translating. For example, you might cough or sneeze to illustrate *cold*.

Dialogue (Page 2)

1. Present the dialogue orally, choosing from the strategies on page 1 of this guide.

2. After students have heard the dialogue twice, check their comprehension with simple questions requiring yes/no or one-word answers. Examples: "Was Pavel sick last week or last month? How is Mike? Who was quite ill, Mike or Mike's mom?"

3. Students may read the dialogue aloud in groups of three, taking the roles of Mike, Luz, and Pavel and then switching until each student has read each part.

4. Construct and conduct pattern practice with these sentences:
   How's your _____? (mother, father, husband, roommate)
   I have a _____. (fever, cold)
   His _____ hurts. (stomach, arm, leg)

He can't _____. (breathe, think, sit, sleep, walk, talk, work, move his arm)

Talking It Over (Page 3)

1. Share a family member's previous health problem or one of your own. Ask about students' experiences with illness.

2. Have students work in pairs so each may tell a partner about his or her present and past states of health.

3. Elicit a variety of responses to the question, "How are you?" Write each different answer on a note card. Add additional common phrases if needed: *horrible, awful, improving, so-so, under the weather, rotten, great, fine, terrific, super, wonderful, excellent*, etc. Have several students sort the note cards, placing them in a continuum from *horrible* to *excellent*, or have students hold one card each and line up in order of increasingly good health. Several students may act out a miraculous recovery, progressing through all the stages of recovery until they are bounding with good health at *super* and *excellent*.

4. Elicit other common ailments in addition to *fever* and *cold*. Examples: *cough, sore throat, headache, toothache, backache*. Use a large diagram of the human body to show which part of the body is affected, or refer to the diagrams on pages 81–82 of the student text.

Working Together (Page 3)

1. Provide cues for class to respond with "I'm sorry to hear that" or "I'm glad to hear that," or "I hope you (he/she) feel(s) better soon.'

   Example: **Teacher:** My sister is sick.
   　　　　　　Class: I'm sorry to hear that.

   Other teacher cues: My brother is in the hospital. My uncle has a fever. My son has a cold. My mother is getting better. My father is feeling ill. My aunt is improving. My friend is in good spirits.

2. Then have members of the class provide cues describing their own health or that of family

and friends. Other students should answer, using responses from number 1 above.

3. Have students work in pairs to write new dialogues based on the cues and responses. Then have students practice the dialogues and perform them for the class.

Real Talk (Page 3)

1. Show by example that the -s and -es endings create plural nouns and singular verbs. Have students create sentences with the words used as examples.

2. Help students distinguish the voiced and voiceless variants of s—the "s" sound in *saw* and the "z" sound in *dogs*.

Putting It Together (Page 4)

1. Present the verb *exercise* with information about yourself, such as: "I never exercise. I exercise once a year. I don't exercise regularly." Have students tell how often they exercise. Introduce frequency words such as *once/twice/three times a day/week/month/year; every day/week/evening/morning*.

2. *Practice A* may be done as a listening exercise (students cover sentences and mark their responses as you read). Alternately, students may read along silently as you read or read silently by themselves.

3. Include practice with *he* and *she* if students have already learned these pronouns and will not be confused. After one person has made a statement about himself or herself, a partner can tell the group about him or her.

4. To facilitate the interviewing in *Practice B*, divide the class into interviewers and interviewees. At the end of five or six minutes, have them switch roles. This may also be done as a class exercise, with students taking turns being the interviewers, recording the information about five interviewees on a chart on the board. When the charts are completed, students can use them to create a paragraph.

Read and Think (Page 5)

1. Before reading, ask, "What do you think is the most common illness? What is the difference between a symptom and a disease? How can a person get an illness?" Introduce the idiom *catch* _____ (a cold, the flu, the measles). Ask, "What is a vaccine? Have you been vaccinated against some diseases?"

2. Refer to the reading strategies on page 3 of this guide.

In Your Community (Page 5)

1. For question 1, help the group decide in advance whom they are going to interview and when they will schedule the interview. Let them role-play in class first.

2. For question 2, have students look at the thermometers and note the differences between Fahrenheit and centigrade. (A conversion table appears on page 84 of the student text. The conversion formulas are $°F = (9/5 °C) + 32$; $°C = 5/9(°F - 32)$.

Warn about the dangers of touching the mercury when a thermometer breaks. New kinds of devices to monitor fevers can be patched under the arm or on the forehead. Bring in any of these that you or students have access to. Demonstrate the proper technique for using a conventional thermometer.

Figuring Out the U.S. (Page 6)

Supply realia such as ads from health clubs and weight loss clubs, No Smoking signs, and nutritional charts. Bring in a pack of cigarettes and point out the Surgeon General's health warning. Use these to illustrate vocabulary, extend awareness, and stimulate additional questions and discussion.

Your Turn (Page 6)

When discussing the questions in **Your Turn**, be alert to possible embarrassment to smokers or overweight persons in the class. Mutual tolerance and respect should be created and maintained.

2 What Can You Recommend?

```
Competency
Asking for recommendations for
over-the-counter preparations or home
remedies

Content Reading
Dosages and precautions on medicine
labels

Cultural Reading
Natural remedies for minor ailments

Structure
Commands

Listening/Speaking Tip
ph as a spelling for the "f" sound
```

Before You Listen (Page 7)

1. Introduce the illustration using the strategies on page 1 of this guide. Have students ask each other additional questions based on the picture.

2. Teach key vocabulary. Clarify meanings without translating. For example, gesture to show *upset stomach* and *swallow*. Draw three lines and point out the middle line to clarify *middle*. Use actual objects to show *tablespoon*, *medicine bottle*, and *label*. Point out *pharmacy* in the illustration.

Dialogue (Page 8)

1. Present the dialogue orally, choosing from the strategies on page 1 of this guide.

2. After the students have heard the dialogue twice, check their comprehension with simple questions requiring yes/no or one-word answers. Examples: "Does Carlos have an upset stomach or a cold? Is Peptaid a medicine? Is it a liquid or pills?"

3. Students may read the dialogue aloud in groups of three, taking the roles of Mike, Carlos, and the pharmacist and then switching until each student has read each part.

4. Construct and conduct pattern drills for the pattern "Excuse me, do you have _____?"

Talking It Over (Page 9)

Tell what a member of your family does when he or she has an upset stomach. Elicit the meaning of *home remedy*. Ask students, "Do you have any home remedies?"

Working Together (Page 9)

1. Explain the difference between *taking* medicine (internal use) and *using* medicine (often external use).

2. Bring in an assortment of over-the-counter medicine bottles and packages. Have students determine what conditions they are intended for. They may role-play an additional dialogue in pairs, using the names of the medications:

Person A: Do you recommend (Feratol) for stomach pain?
Person B: I don't know. I've never tried it.

Real Talk (Page 9)

Elicit additional *ph* words from students, such as *phantom*, *phrase*, and *phobia*.

Putting It Together (Page 10)

1. For *Practice A*, explain that the implied subject of an imperative sentence is *you*, and that imperative sentences are exceptions to the standard pattern of subject + predicate.

2. In *Practice B*, be sure students understand that they are to use command (imperative) forms rather than forms with *should*.

Read and Think (Page 11)

1. Bring in realia such as headache remedies, cough syrups, and nose drops. Point out the labels. Ask, "What questions does a label answer?" (Possible answers: "What is the product for? How much should you take and how often? When should you take it, and

how? Are there any dangers? Who should not take it? When should you not take it? What is the expiration date?")

2. If any of the products has a childproof cap, point out the label on the bottle. Point out the words *DIRECTIONS*, *INDICATIONS*, and *WARNINGS* on the labels. Ask students to come up with a definition for each word.

3. Refer to the reading strategies on page 3 of this guide. After students answer the questions in their text, help them compose additional questions to ask each other based on the reading.

4. Have students work in small groups telling their experiences with medications.

In Your Community (Page 11)

1. For question 1, elicit or teach the structures they may need in order to speak with the pharmacist. Have students role-play talking to the pharmacist in class.

2. Invite a pharmacist to visit your class. Work with students to brainstorm a list of questions to ask the pharmacist.

Figuring Out the U.S. (Page 12)

1. Talk about natural remedies without endorsing any of them. Provide a recipe for chicken soup and ask students why many people use it as a "first line of defense" against a cold.

2. Ask students if they can get remedies from their native countries at local stores. Make a chart on the board with the approximate location of each store and the remedies available there.

Your Turn (Page 12)

Stress the importance of students' being responsible for their own health choices. Discuss how they can determine whether a remedy may have side effects. For example, a food such as chicken soup is likely to be harmless, even if it may not be as effective in healing. What intermediate steps are available between a natural remedy and a trip to the doctor's office? (Possible answers: ask a pharmacist's advice; take an over-the-counter medication.)

3 Have You Been to Our Office?

Competency
Making an appointment by telephone

Content Reading
A health form

Cultural Reading
Comparing private doctors and clinics

Structure
Wh-questions: *when*

Listening/Speaking Tip
Repeating telephone numbers

Before You Listen (Page 13)

1. Introduce the illustration using the strategies on page 1 of this guide. Have students create and ask additional questions based on the picture.

2. Ask students to share experiences about making an appointment or going to a doctor's office.

3. Teach key vocabulary such as *doctor's office, receptionist, appointment, evening hours, terrible, pain,* and *corner.* Clarify meanings without translating. For example, use body language to show *pain in the stomach.*

Dialogue (Page 14)

1. Present the dialogue orally, choosing from the strategies on page 1 of this guide.

2. After students have heard the dialogue twice, check their comprehension with simple questions requiring yes/no or one-word answers. Examples: "Has Carlos been to see Dr. Alamo before? Does Carlos work in the daytime or at night? Is next Thursday at seven all right? Is eight o'clock tomorrow all right?"

3. Construct and conduct pattern practice for these patterns:
   I want to make an appointment with _____.
   I have a terrible pain in my ____.
   We'll see you tomorrow at ___ o'clock.

Talking It Over (Page 15)

1. Tell about any experience you have had with misunderstanding an appointment time.

2. Ask students questions such as: "Have you made appointments by telephone? What questions did the other person ask? Have you had problems with errors? How can the errors be avoided?"

3. Mention the fact that in the United States, doctors expect patients to arrive at the precise appointment time and that doctors often charge for missed appointments. Point out, however, that doctors sometimes keep patients waiting for over an hour, even if the patient comes on time. Ask students why they think the doctor's time seems to be more important than the patient's.

Working Together (Page 15)

Brainstorm additional questions with the class and write them on the board. Then have pairs of students role-play conversations based on the questions.

Real Talk (Page 15)

1. Dictate times for several students to write on the blackboard as others write them at their desks. Slowly increase the speed and the complexity as the students become more accurate. Repeat the procedure with addresses.

2. Have pairs of students practice making appointments, with one person repeating the time and the address given by his or her partner. Use local addresses. Urge students to ask for clarification if they don't understand.

Putting It Together (Page 16)

1. Review question forms with *can, will, do, does, did,* etc. Introduce the question word *when* as a general time word. Contrast it with *what time,* which is more specific.

2. After practicing with *when,* present questions with *where* and *how.* Then have students create questions with *when, where,* and *how.*

Read and Think (Page 17)

1. This exercise will require careful translation using good bilingual dictionaries or consulting bilingual health professionals. Stress to students that although they are encouraged to guess word meanings in some situations, it is very important that they know the exact English word for any serious illnesses they may have had. Work as a group and discuss any discrepancies in translation of the names of illnesses. However, be sensitive to students who prefer not to reveal their medical histories. Some students may wish to complete this exercise individually.

2. Have students look up any additional illnesses they have had or know of and add these words to the list.

In Your Community (Page 17)

1. Invite a health professional to speak to your class about the importance of checkups and keeping an accurate health history. Discuss how to determine if a doctor is good.

2. Invite a nontraditional health professional such as an herbalist, acupuncturist, or chiropractor to explain the theory of healing according to his or her training.

Figuring Out the U.S. (Page 18)

1. Ask students whether they go to private doctors, clinics, HMOs, or elsewhere. If some students prefer not to go to traditional doctors, ask them why. Encourage students to express their opinions.

2. As a class, make a chart comparing clinics and private practitioners. Have students name similarities and differences.

3. Explain that twenty years ago, some private doctors made house calls, but stress that this rarely happens today. Ask students if doctors or healers in their native countries make home visits. If they do, ask students to describe these visits.

Your Turn (Page 18)

As a class, generate a list of ways to find a doctor. Then discuss the advantages and disadvantages of each method.

> Refer to page 62 of this guide for teaching suggestions for Review Unit One.

4 Show Me Where the Pain Is

> **Competency**
> Understanding and responding to a doctor's questions
>
> **Content Reading**
> Symptoms of common health problems
>
> **Cultural Reading**
> Involvement in health care
>
> **Structure**
> Irregular past-tense verbs
>
> **Listening/Speaking Tip**
> Initial consonant blends

Before You Listen (Page 21)

1. Introduce the illustration using the strategies on page 1 of this guide. Have the students ask each other additional questions about the picture.

2. Teach key vocabulary such as *examination*, *pain*, *abdomen*, *tongue*, and *how long*. Clarify meanings without translating. For example, demonstrate *stick out your tongue*.

Dialogue (Page 22)

1. Present the dialogue orally, choosing from the strategies on page 1 of this guide.

2. After students have heard the dialogue twice, check their comprehension with simple questions requiring yes/no or one-word answers. Examples: "Where is Carlos? Why did he go to the doctor?"

3. Students may read the dialogue aloud in pairs, taking the roles of Dr. Alamo and Carlos and then switching until each student has read each part.

Talking It Over (Page 23)

Ask the students what they think the doctor is looking for when he checks Carlos's lungs, heart, blood pressure, and abdomen.

Working Together (Page 23)

1. Before presenting this exercise, teach names of common symptoms. Also review *fever*, *cold*, *cough*, *sore throat*, *headache*, *toothache*, and *backache*.

2. Students contribute answers to the conversation as the teacher or an advanced student writes the lines of dialogue on the board. Then students work in pairs and write their own answers. Have them practice the dialogue they created—first with the text, then from memory.

Real Talk (Page 23)

1. Speakers of different languages will have varying difficulties with these consonant blends. For example, Spanish speakers will tend to precede *st* and other *s* combinations with an additional vowel sound. First they will have to hear the difference between *esteem* and *steam*. Model the production of *st-* words until they can reproduce the "st" sound without a preceding vowel.

2. Some speakers of Asian languages will find combinations with *r* difficult. After the students repeat the isolated sounds that you model, put the sounds back into a relevant context.

Putting It Together (Page 25)

1. Review past tenses of regular verbs and teach the past tenses of irregular verbs needed to complete the exercise. Explain how to form questions and negative sentences.

2. Elicit the past forms of additional verbs. Circulate around the room as students work in pairs and provide students with any additional past forms needed. Point out the chart of irregular verbs on page 83 of the student text.

3. Have students play "Team Tic-Tac-Toe" with irregular verbs. The game is described on page 2 of this guide.

4. In future dialogues and reading lessons, point out the past and basic forms of verbs.

Read and Think (Page 25)

1. Bring a selection of home medical guidebooks from the library for students to browse through. Find any charts such as the one on page 25 or other forms of listing symptoms, possible diagnoses, and indications. *Listen to Your Body* (Ellen Michaud *et al.*, Emmaus, Pa.: Rodale Press, Inc., 1988) has a very useful explanation of the relationships among symptoms, possible causes, and likely medical treatments. It also indicates which symptoms require immediate medical attention.

2. Point out that *-itis* means *inflamed*. Other examples are *tonsillitis, bursitis, arthritis*.

3. Discuss what *contagious* means. Point out the silent *p* in *pneumonia*.

4. Explain that a rash is a symptom that has many possible causes—heat; illness, such as measles, chicken pox, rubella, or roseola; fungus; allergy to food, clothing, or deodorant and other chemicals—and that only a doctor can accurately tell the cause of a rash.

5. Have students practice reporting symptoms using the following patterns:
I have a _____. (rash, fever, headache, sore throat, pain in my chest)
I've been _____ a lot. (coughing, wheezing, vomiting)

In Your Community (Page 25)

Most hospitals have a variety of health services for their patients and the public. These may include postoperative discussion groups and classes on preventing heart attacks, controlling weight problems, and quitting smoking.

Figuring Out the U.S. (Page 26)

1. Have students name specific problems and the questions they would want to ask a doctor about these problems.

2. Ask which illnesses are contagious. Talk about different means of transmitting disease: sneezing; coughing; hand contact; kissing; sharing utensils, towels, or clothes; restaurant workers' not washing hands; sex; bleeding; blood transfusions; contaminated needles; and so on.

3. Ask, "What can you do to avoid spreading a contagious disease? What is done in your native country?" Point out that in some parts of the world, people wear gauze masks when they have a cold to prevent spreading it to others.

Your Turn (Page 26)

Discuss the added difficulties of a limited-English speaker dealing with an English-only doctor.

5 We'll Have to Run Some Tests

> **Competency**
> Asking questions to ensure accurate understanding of advice
>
> **Content Reading**
> Prescriptions and labels on prescription medicine
>
> **Cultural Reading**
> Alternative health care practitioners
>
> **Structure**
> Future with *going to*
>
> **Listening/Speaking Tip**
> Polysyllabic names of medical specialists

Before You Listen (Page 27)

1. Introduce the illustration using the strategies on page 1 of this guide. Ask, "What other tests might Dr. Alamo do?"

2. Teach key vocabulary such as *blood sample*, *cotton*, *radiologist*, *X-ray*, *risks*, and *fee*. Clarify meanings without translating. For example, use actual objects to show *cotton* and *X-ray*.

Dialogue (Page 28)

1. Present the dialogue orally, choosing from the strategies on page 1 of this guide.

2. After students have heard the dialogue twice, check their comprehension with simple questions requiring yes/no or one-word answers. Examples: "Did Carlos have a blood test or an English test? Will he need an X-ray of his stomach or his head? Is Dr. Alamo a radiologist? Does a radiologist take blood tests or X-rays?"

3. Students may read the dialogue aloud in pairs, taking the roles of Carlos and Dr. Alamo and then switching until each student has read each part.

4. Construct and conduct pattern practice with these patterns:
   Are you going to do that _____? (right now, tomorrow, next week, tonight, next time)
   Is it going to _____ a lot? (cost, hurt, bleed)

Discuss the fee with the _____. (doctor, radiologist, dentist, nurse, cardiologist, gynecologist, pediatrician)

Talking It Over (Page 29)

Have students make a list of medical tests they or members of their family have had. They should also list the specialists who did the tests and, if possible, the cost. Be sensitive to students who are not comfortable sharing this information.

Working Together (Page 29)

Students generate the conversation as the teacher or an advanced student writes it on the board. A sample conversation follows.

Doctor: I have to run some tests.
Patient: What tests?
Doctor: First, I need a blood sample.
Patient: What will the blood test show?
Doctor: It will show if you have enough iron.

Real Talk (Page 29)

Elicit the meanings of the names of these specialists if the students know them. Add any other specialists the students know and work on those pronunciations as well.

Putting It Together (Page 30)

1. Point out that the present continuous form of the verb *to go* is used with the basic form of other verbs to create one of the two future tenses in English.

2. For *Practice A*, elicit additional sample sentences to write on the board to illustrate students' expected actions in the future.

3. For *Practice B*, examples include: "When am I going to need the operation? Is it going to be painful? Will I have to stay in the hospital a long time? Is it going to cost a lot? Will I be able to walk soon? Is it major surgery?" Discuss some of the differences between major and minor surgery. (Major surgery often requires general anesthesia and a hospital stay.)

Read and Think (Page 31)

1. Bring in used prescription bottles as realia. Also supply tablets, pills, and capsules to distinguish the shapes. Always exercise caution when displaying drugs.

2. The prescription form in the student text is to be read by a pharmacist, not by the student. It is partly in Latin. Students may want to know the meanings of the abbreviations and Latin words (DOB = date of birth, RX = prescribed, diem = day).

3. Let students know that in some situations a doctor will call in a prescription to their local drugstore. Have them find out if their local drugstore makes deliveries.

4. Discuss the difference between brand-name medicines and generic brands. (Brand-name medicines cost more because they are advertised; the generic equivalent may be slightly different from the brand-name medicine.)

5. Explain that pharmacists can give useful information about medications, including possible side effects, but make it clear that only doctors can prescribe medicine. Ask students if there are pharmacies in their native countries. If so, ask them what the pharmacist can and cannot do.

In Your Community (Page 31)

Invite a health professional in to talk about AIDS—symptoms, tests, contagion, prevention, and treatment.

Figuring Out the U.S. (Page 32)

1. Point out that people often get sick, take nothing, and get well. A scab forms over a cut and later falls off. Ask, "What is the source of this healing when no medicine is used?"

2. Discuss the placebo effect (a sick person gets better when given a treatment, even though the treatment has no medicinal value). What is the source of this healing?

Your Turn (Page 32)

1. If you feel the subject matter is appropriate, discuss the dilemma faced by some cancer patients: Should they follow an orthodox course of treatment (surgery to remove a tumor, and then radiation or chemotherapy) with some serious side effects? Or should they elect unorthodox treatments with fewer side effects, such as diet modification or megavitamin therapy? Stress the need to thoroughly investigate the risks and success rates of suggested treatments when faced with such decisions.

2. Another question concerns conflicts between a person's religion and the state. Some religions do not permit blood transfusions, for example. Should a person be allowed to die if a blood transfusion would save his or her life?

6 Look At This Bill!

Before You Listen (Page 33)

1. Introduce the illustration using the strategies on page 1 of this guide. Have the students create additional questions to ask each other based on the picture.

2. Teach key vocabulary such as *bill*, *insurance*, *receipt*, *claim form*, and *reimburse*. Clarify meanings without translating. For example, act out the concept *reimburse*. Have one student be the doctor, one the patient, and one the insurance representative: the patient gives the doctor a check for $70, the doctor gives him a receipt, and the patient gives the receipt and a claim form to the insurance representative, who reimburses him with a check for $56. Point out that insurance rarely covers 100 percent of a medical bill.

Dialogue (Page 34)

1. Present the dialogue orally, choosing from the strategies on page 1 of this guide.

2. After students have heard the dialogue twice, check their comprehension with simple questions requiring yes/no or one-word answers. Examples: "Did Carlos go to the doctor or to the dentist? How much is the bill? Is Carlos happy? Did he have to pay the doctor right away? Does he have insurance? Does he know how it works?"

3. Students may read the dialogue aloud in pairs, taking the roles of Carlos, Mike, and the personnel manager and then switching until each student has read each part.

4. Construct and conduct pattern practice with this pattern: Does the policy cover _____? (blood tests, X-rays, ambulance service, private nurses, outpatient care, emergency room service, chiropractors)

Talking It Over (Page 35)

Have students create and discuss additional questions based on the dialogue and on their personal experiences with medical bills and insurance.

Working Together (Page 35)

Help students create additional questions and answers to finish the conversation.
Example:

> **Mike:** Will the insurance pay for ambulance service?
>
> **Personnel manager:** I think so. Let me check.

Then have students work in pairs to practice the dialogue.

Real Talk (Page 35)

1. When students have discovered the rule that *c* is "soft" (like *s*) before *i* and *e*, and "hard" in most other positions, have them create columns of words that contain the hard and soft "c" sounds. Start with words from page 35 of the student text, as shown below:

Hard C	Soft C
cover	office
cross	policy

2. They may also notice that sometimes *ch* is pronounced like "k" and sometimes like "ch." After *s* or before *r* it is often pronounced with the "k" sound: *school*, *schedule*, *Christian*. But other times there is no rule: *charity*, *chart*, *character*.

Putting It Together (Page 36)

Point out that the difference between the two futures is slight, and in many cases they are interchangeable.

I'm going to do it later.
I will do it later.

The distinction is that *will* may imply more of a commitment to do the action in the future.

Read and Think (Page 37)

1. Ask students if they think insurance policies should cover all medical expenses. Ask how they think this should affect the cost of the policies.

2. This exercise may be difficult because of unfamiliar vocabulary. Take time to be sure students are comfortable with the terms that even native English speakers have trouble with. Use student experiences to illustrate key concepts such as *deductible*, *covered charges*, *allowance*, and *exclusions*.

In Your Community (Page 37)

1. For question 1, compare the costs of preventive medicine—a flu shot, for instance—versus the cost of getting the flu, absence from work, and possible complications. Remind students of side effects from flu shots and the risk factors of age and health. Ask, "Who do you think should get flu shots?"

2. For question 2, discuss the reasons for the high cost of medical procedures and insurance: expensive equipment; modern breakthrough techniques such as heart transplants; keeping people in comas alive through respirators, even if those people would ordinarily have died; and saving premature babies with high-tech equipment at a cost of thousands of dollars a day. Discuss the effects of the increasing cost of health care.

Figuring Out the U.S. (Page 38)

Help students fill out the application for their entire family. Elicit the definitions for *annually*, *semiannually*, *quarterly*, and *monthly*.

Your Turn (Page 38)

1. Have students make a chart depicting the kinds of health plans available for residents of the countries represented in the class. Use a chart like the one below:

Country	Costs Paid by	Quality of Care	Efficiency of Care

2. If students were to design a country's health-care system, what elements would they include? For instance, who would pay to educate doctors? How much would doctors be paid? Who would make the decisions about a patient getting extraordinary and very expensive care, such as a heart transplant, that might only provide a short time of added life? What other issues would a planner have to take into consideration? Ask students to give reasons for their answers.

Refer to page 62 of this guide for teaching suggestions for Review Unit Two.

7 We Can't Pay the Doctor's Bills

> **Competency**
> Inquiring about government health-assistance programs
>
> **Content Reading**
> Medicaid and Medicare
>
> **Cultural Reading**
> Bureaucracies and red tape
>
> **Structure**
> Verbs that take gerunds/Verbs that take infinitives
>
> **Listening/Speaking Tip**
> Two sounds for the letter *g*

Before You Listen (Page 41)

1. Introduce the illustration using the strategies on page 1 of this guide. Have students imagine the conversation between Olga and the clerk.

2. Introduce the concept of government-funded health programs. Teach key vocabulary such as *eligible, unemployed, earnings, apply, disabled, resident,* and *county*. Clarify meanings without translating. For example, show an application form and offer it to a student to fill out to illustrate *apply*; point to Olga's stomach to illustrate *expecting a baby*.

Dialogue (Page 42)

1. Present the dialogue orally, choosing from the strategies on page 1 of this guide.

2. After students have heard the dialogue twice, check their comprehension with simple questions requiring yes/no or one-word answers. Examples: "Is Medicare for pregnant women or for people over 65? Is Medicare the same as Medicaid? Is Olga a resident of the country or the county? Does she have children? Does she have a job? Is her husband employed?"

3. Students may read the dialogue aloud in pairs, taking the roles of Olga and the clerk and then switching until each student has read both parts.

4. Create and conduct pattern practice with these patterns:

   I'd like to apply for _____. (Medicare, Medicaid, welfare, Social Security, a job, a driver's license)

   I work as a _____. (waitress, machinist, mechanic, reporter, nurse, teacher, clerk, secretary, doctor)

   We can't afford _____. (the doctor's bills, a new car, a larger apartment, the tuition, the telephone bill)

Talking It Over (Page 43)

1. After students have worked in pairs discussing the questions, have them tell the class how people deal with health costs and payments in their native countries. For example, does a patient see a doctor without paying anything or does the patient pay the doctor and then get reimbursed by the government?

2. Have students tell about attitudes in their native countries regarding women working, pregnant women working, and career women versus homemakers. Ask questions such as: "How fast are traditions changing? What is bringing about these changes?"

Working Together (Page 43)

Allow students to come up with their own questions (additional suggested questions: "Do I need my children's birth certificates? Can I qualify if I have a part-time job? Can I qualify if my husband lives with me?").

Real Talk (Page 43)

You may introduce two other sounds of the letter *g*: "ng" as in *bring* and "zh" as in *garage* (American pronunciation).

Putting It Together (Page 44)

1. Talk about something that you enjoy and something that you plan to do. Write the sentences on the board. For example: *I enjoy teaching. I plan to teach at this school next year.*

2. Point out that some verbs are followed by the gerund or present participle form (*e.g., enjoy/ dislike/adore teaching*) and some verbs are followed by the infinitive form (*e.g., plan/ hope/want to teach*).

3. For students who have not been exposed to this distinction, teach verbs followed by the gerund on one day and verbs followed by infinitives on another day. If you attempt to teach both the same day, they will stay mixed in the students' minds forever!

4. Point out that some verbs take either the gerund or the infinitive depending on whether a subject is mentioned:

   She allows **smoking** in the dining room.

   She allows people **to smoke** in the dining room.

5. *Practice A* can be a simple task if students are allowed to look at the lists above the exercise to select the correct word. More advanced students can test their listening skills by choosing the form that "sounds right." One thing they should *not* trust is direct translation from the patterns used in their native languages.

6. For *Practice B*, give oral practice before turning students on their own. Have them do a controlled practice drill first, using verbs that take the gerund:

   Do you **allow** smoking in your house? (enjoy, avoid, continue, appreciate, tolerate, consider, despise, excuse, forbid, keep, mind, resent, suggest)

   Then drill with verbs using the infinitive:

   Did you **need** to work? (agree, aim, choose, deserve, desire, forget, prepare, pretend, refuse, wish)

Read and Think (Page 45)

Point out that even Americans are confused at first with the terms *Medicare* and *Medicaid*. While both are national programs, Medicaid is regulated by the states, and each state may have slightly different eligibility guidelines and cut-offs.

In Your Community (Page 45)

1. Divide the class into research groups. Prepare them for the possible difficulty of reaching the right offices. Have students read **Figuring Out the U.S.** on page 46 of the student text prior to calling or visiting the government office as mentioned in question 1.

2. Elicit or teach the question forms the students will need to use, and have them role-play the questions in pairs before doing the research. Assist students in planning and scheduling their calls.

3. If possible, invite a social worker or community information officer to explain the application procedure, eligibility rules, and other details of working with Medicaid.

Figuring Out the U.S. (Page 46)

Wrap a pile of papers with a red ribbon. Explain that in England a few hundred years ago, lawyers and government workers tied their official papers with red tape. It was difficult to get something out that had been tied, as each bundle had to be cut. Thus, we have the expression *go through a lot of red tape*, which means *have a lot of difficulty getting results*.

Your Turn (Page 46)

1. This topic may be sensitive for some students who wish to keep confidential the fact that they are receiving public aid. Others may be quite open about the difficulties or successes in applying for and receiving public assistance. Some may have heated opinions about the matter. Ask students if they think society should be responsible for ensuring the health of its citizens.

2. Have students select one of the questions and write their opinion. One possible assignment is for students to write letters to friends in their native countries describing any dealings they have had with federal, state, or local government offices in the United States.

8 This Is an Emergency!

Before You Listen (Page 47)

1. Introduce the illustration using the strategies on page 1 of this guide. Ask, "How do you think this happened? What hazards were there?" Have students ask each other additional questions about the scene.

2. Teach key vocabulary such as *accident*, *emergency*, *ambulance*, *injury*, *unconscious*, *neck*, *spine*, *relative*, and *neighbor*. Clarify meanings without translating. For example, use a real or imaginary telephone, and speak with urgency to illustrate *emergency*. Point to your *neck* and *spine*.

Dialogue (Page 48)

1. Present the dialogue orally, choosing from the strategies on page 1 of this guide.

2. After students have heard the dialogue twice, check their comprehension with simple questions requiring yes/no or one-word answers. Examples: "Did Mike call an ambulance or a doctor? Did Pavel get hit by a car or fall on the ice? Is he conscious? Will an ambulance or a police car come in five minutes? Is Mike a relative or a neighbor? Will Mike call Pavel's son or his daughter?"

3. Students may read the dialogue aloud in pairs, taking the roles of Mike and the dispatcher and then switching until each student has read both parts.

4. Have students review saying and spelling out their addresses in a clear and understandable fashion.

5. Construct and conduct pattern practice with these patterns:

   (He/she) broke (his/her) _____. (leg, arm, neck, foot)

Talking It Over (Page 49)

1. Talk about any experience you have had with an ambulance and elicit personal experiences from the class.

2. Ask, "Why should you pull over to the side of the road when you hear an ambulance siren? Why do ambulances have *ambulance* written in reverse writing on the front of the vehicle?"

Working Together (Page 49)

Students may need to review the present continuous tense before describing the scene. Expected patterns: "There was a crash. A car is burning. A man is pulling someone out of the car. A woman is lying on the grass." Students may need to review prepositions such as *out of*, *from*, *near*, *next to*. Work with the whole group before having students work in pairs for additional practice.

Real Talk (Page 49)

Demonstrate the distinction between the short "a" as in *map* and the short "o" as in *mop*. Many languages do not distinguish between these sounds. Show that there is a greater tension and a smaller mouth opening, as well as lips pulled back, to make the short "a" sound.

Putting It Together (Page 50)

1. Draw a line on the board and explain that it is a time line. Make a star in the center of the line, and label it NOW. Make a slash to indicate an event in the past. Explain that the simple past indicates that something happened at a specific time in the past. Describe a sequence of past events, and make sure students understand the simple past before you proceed. Then say that we use the past-continuous tense if something else was happening when a past action occurred. Draw a wavy line under the time line at the point of the past action to indicate ongoing action at a time in the past. Use examples from the class at the moment. For example: *I was teaching when José walked in the room.*

2. Give more practice with the past continuous tense by asking questions such as: "What were you doing at 6 A.M. (8 A.M., noon, 3 P.M., 7 P.M.) yesterday?" Demonstrate, by means of the time line, that the exact time is like a point in the past and that the action was going on before, during, and possibly after that point.

Read and Think (Page 51)

1. Clarify vocabulary after students have guessed at meanings using clues from the context. To clarify *next of kin*, have students tell who their next of kin is. Students should carry this person's name, address, and telephone number to notify in case of emergency.

2. Have students make a list of possible problems that a typical emergency room would have to respond to. Students may role-play being accident victims and "doctors" who will question them (or their companions) and make decisions about whom to treat first.

In Your Community (Page 51)

1. For question 3, help students formulate the questions they will be asking and role-play the inquiry in class before they try it outside.

2. Invite a local ambulance worker or emergency medical worker to talk about his or her job and experiences. You might also invite a person qualified to explain and demonstrate the Heimlich maneuver, artificial resuscitation, CPR, and other emergency first-aid procedures.

Figuring Out the U.S. (Page 52)

Tell of any experiences you have had in an emergency room and elicit personal experiences from your students. Clarify any vocabulary after students have guessed meanings from the context.

Your Turn (Page 52)

Have students reread the **Your Turn** questions. Ask students whether or not each question would make a good writing topic. (Some of the questions may not be appropriate, since they yield very short answers.) Have students give reasons for their choices. Then have students select one of the questions and write their opinion.

9 Which Tooth Is Bothering You?

Competencies
Asking questions about dental care and treatment

Content Reading
Dental care

Cultural Reading
Painless dental techniques

Structure
Should

Listening/Speaking Tip
The "v" sound

Before You Listen (Page 53)

1. Introduce the illustration using the strategies on page 1 of this guide. Encourage students to talk about what they see in the picture.

2. Teach key vocabulary such as *dentist*, *tooth*, *cavity*, *drill*, *root*, and *nerve*. Clarify meanings without translating. For example, draw a tooth with two long roots and point to the *root* and *nerve*.

Dialogue (Page 54)

1. Present the dialogue orally, choosing from the strategies on page 1 of this guide.

2. After students have heard the dialogue twice, check their comprehension with simple questions requiring yes/no or one-word answers. Examples: "Is there a cavity in Mike's tooth? Does the dentist want to pull the tooth or save it? How often should people have their teeth checked?"

3. Students may read the dialogue aloud in pairs, taking the roles of Mike and Dr. Ford and then switching until each student has read both parts.

4. Find a diagram of a tooth in an encyclopedia. Copy the diagram onto the board and label these parts: *crown*, *root*, *enamel*, *nerve*, *gum*, *jawbone*.

5. Construct and conduct pattern practice with these patterns: It's easier to ___ than to ___. (fill a small cavity/fill a large one; speak/write; read/spell)

6. Explain that Dr. Ford is a D.D.S. (Doctor of Dental Surgery) while Dr. Alamo is an M.D. (Doctor of Medicine). Other kinds of doctors are D.C. (Doctor of Chiropractic), D.O. (Doctor of Osteopathy), Ph.D. (Doctor of Philosophy), and Ed.D. (Doctor of Education).

Talking It Over (Page 55)

Ask additional questions such as: "Have you ever had a root canal? How long did it take? Was it painful? Did you get novocaine? How did that feel? Were there any side effects? Do you still have the tooth?"

Working Together (Page 55)

As a class, brainstorm additional questions for the conversations. Some possibilities: "Will there be side effects from the anesthetic? What will happen if I don't have the root canal done?"

Real Talk (Page 55)

1. Present additional words to illustrate the sound of the letter *v*: *very, victor, valuable; save silver*—it's *very valuable*; the *cavity* has reached the *nerve*.

2. Have students work with minimal pairs as shown below.

A. If your students do not make a distinction between the "b" and "v" sounds, practice these pairs:

Initial Position		Medial Position	
very	berry	covered	cupboard
vest	best	marvel	marble
vote	boat	calves	cabs

Final Position	
rove	robe
curve	curb

B. If your students make the sound "w" instead of "v," practice these pairs:

we'll	veal	wiper	viper
wet	vet	worse	verse
wine	vine	why	vie

Make two columns of words: one column with the "v" sound and one column with the "b" sound. (Use the "w" and "v" sounds for the second group of students.) Select words your students know from the lists on page 54 of this guide or illustrate the words. To develop their listening competence in distinguishing the two sounds, say one of the pair of words and have students raise one finger if it is in column one and two fingers if in column two. When students can hear the difference, they are ready to say the difference. Show them the position of the upper teeth on the lower lip to produce the "v" sound. Suggest that students use a mirror when practicing at home.

Putting It Together (Page 56)

1. Discuss dental hygiene. Refer to the picture on page 56 of the student text for vocabulary words such as *floss* and *brush*.

2. Bring in food charts and magazine pictures of foods and drinks. Define *junk foods* as foods containing a lot of sugar or salt, lots of calories, and little nutritional value.

3. Do an experiment: Put a tooth in a glass of soda and leave it for a few days. Observe the results.

Read and Think (Page 57)

1. Elicit the many purposes of teeth: chewing, speaking, self-defense, cutting, and so on. Ask students what they think a natural tooth is worth. Ask, "What is a finger worth? Is a finger more valuable than a tooth? Would a false finger be a good substitute for a missing real finger?"

2. Clarify any new vocabulary items after students have guessed their meanings from the context.

In Your Community (Page 57)

Invite a dentist, dental hygienist, or other dental professional to speak to the class. Help students prepare questions in advance. Ask about tooth care, gum disease (gingivitis, periodontitis), and the dangers of human bites.

Figuring Out the U.S. (Page 58)

Have students paraphrase each paragraph after clarifying vocabulary. Ask, "Do you have a dentist here in the United States? Where is the dentist's office located? Is your dentist a painless dentist?"

Your Turn (Page 58)

Continue the discussion of the value of one's natural teeth. Ask students what they would do if they had no money and were told that they would lose a finger if they didn't treat an infection: Would they borrow money to save the finger? Would they borrow money to save a tooth?

Refer to page 62 of this guide for teaching suggestions for Review Unit Three.

10 Do You Worry Much?

```
Competency
Describing emotional states

Content Reading
Types of professional and self-help groups

Cultural Reading
Seeking help for emotional difficulties

Structure
Frequency words

Listening/Speaking Tip
Words spelled with silent p
```

Before You Listen (Page 61)

1. Introduce the illustration using the strategies on page 1 of this guide. Ask, "What items are in the picture? Why do you think there are tissues on the table next to Carlos? Do you think stomach problems can come from worry? Do you think Carlos will be able to talk about his problems with a woman?"

2. Teach key vocabulary such as *stress, anxiety, worries, nightmares, familiar,* and *control.* Clarify meanings without translating.

3. Seeking help from counselors and therapists may not be a common practice in some students' native countries. Allow time for any discussion that arises before proceeding with the dialogue. Point out that in areas where extended families live together, there may be less need for professional help because there is always someone who can listen and give advice. The combination of urban living, distance from the extended family, frequent moves, and general culture shock may account for more severe problems than students experienced in their native countries. Social workers and therapists are trained to be good listeners and to help people find their own solutions to problems.

Dialogue (Page 62)

1. Present the dialogue orally, choosing from the strategies on page 1 of this guide.

2. After students have heard the dialogue twice, check their comprehension with simple questions requiring yes/no or one-word answers. Examples: "Does Carlos sleep well? Does he have nightmares?"

3. Students may read the dialogue aloud in pairs, taking the roles of Carlos and Ms. Wendon and then switching until each student has read both parts.

Talking It Over (Page 63)

Students may have many stories to relate regarding stress, nightmares, and related ills since coming to the United States. The expression of their experiences may serve as good support to other students. Some students may not wish to share their worries or appear vulnerable in a group where there is no guarantee of confidentiality. For instance, the worries of an undocumented immigrant must necessarily be kept private. Others may not wish to reveal that they see a counselor or therapist.

Working Together (Page 63)

Introduce frequency words. Have students complete **Putting It Together** on page 64 of the student text before doing this exercise.

Real Talk (Page 63)

Point out that the prefix *psycho-* means *mind* or *spirit* (not *crazy*). Invite the students to check their bilingual dictionaries for other words beginning with this prefix.

Putting It Together (Page 64)

1. Elicit from students things that occur in their lives always, sometimes, never, and so on. Ask, "What are some things that *always* happen in your family?"

2. List the frequency words on page 64 of the student text in a continuum on the board. Say, "If the train is *always* late, we are saying that the train is late 100 percent of the time. What if the train is usually late? What percent would you give to *usually*?" Have students supply a percentage for each frequency word.

Point out that these percentages reflect general guesses and are relative to the thing you are talking about. For example, if an area had three or four hurricanes a year, (*i.e.,* less than one percent of the time), you could still say "They frequently have hurricanes" because many other places never have hurricanes at all.

3. In negative sentences, the position of the frequency word may vary.

   I don't **usually** take vitamins.
   I **usually** don't take vitamins.
   Usually I don't take vitamins.
   I don't take vitamins **usually**.

4. For *Practice B*, circulate about the room and monitor the conversations. Remind students to use the frequency words rather than a specific number of times. Contrast the frequency words' vagueness with the exactness of expressions such as *three times a year*, *twice a week*, and *once a day*.

Read and Think (Page 65)

1. Relate any stories you have about people who got help with handling stress, overcoming fears, changing habits, solving family problems, or healing physical disorders through counseling or self-help groups. Include stories of people who did not benefit from treatment and sought other ways of handling their problems.

2. Clarify any words unknown to your students after they have had a chance to guess at meanings from the context.

In Your Community (Page 65)

1. Bring in telephone books, both white and yellow pages. Have students practice asking for brochures describing the services and treatments provided at each facility mentioned in question 1. After students make the calls, have them report back to the class.

2. Have a professional counselor or member of a self-help organization speak to the class. Have the class prepare questions. One question might be about cost and time for treatment.

Figuring Out the U.S. (Page 66)

1. Relate stories you have about the disappearing stigma attached to getting help from counselors. (You may have to teach the word *stigma*.) Explain that people are more open about their fears and problems: Most American schools have the services of school psychologists; movie stars and public personalities talk about their therapy on television talk shows. Also ask students if *they* think the stigma of therapy is disappearing. If students have American friends and co-workers, ask them how their friends and co-workers feel about therapy.

2. Have students figure the cost of professional psychotherapy at $75 an hour for once a week for two years. Have them discuss the possible value to a person suffering from phobias, nightmares, or stomach pains. (You might also mention that short-term, low-cost therapy is available in some communities.)

3. Bring in information about Marriage Encounter (through the Catholic Church), Smokenders, Alcoholics Anonymous, Adult Children of Alcoholics, and other reputable groups. Discuss the pros and cons of going to these kinds of groups.

Your Turn (Page 66)

1. Point out that there are therapists who are incompetent and can do more harm than good. Just as you should not give medical advice, you also should not make blanket recommendations for therapy.

2. Have students select one of the questions and write their own opinion about it, presenting arguments for their opinion.

11 That's Why It's Called Labor

> **Competency**
> Asking for and understanding prenatal-care advice
>
> **Content Reading**
> Tests during pregnancy
>
> **Cultural Reading**
> Birthing rooms and midwives
>
> **Structure**
> Comparative forms
>
> **Listening/Speaking Tip**
> Two sounds for *th*

Before You Listen (Page 67)

1. Introduce the illustration using the strategies on page 1 of this guide. Ask, "Do you have children? Were they born here or in your native country? Were they born in a hospital or at home?"

2. Teach key vocabulary such as *childbirth*, *labor*, *delivery room*, and *prenatal checkups*. Clarify meanings without translating.

3. Allow longer discussion times for relating personal experiences in pairs if you have many mothers in the class. Give the men equal time to tell of their wives' pregnancies and deliveries or, if they are not fathers, anything told to them about their own births.

Dialogue (Page 68)

1. Present the dialogue orally, choosing from the strategies on page 1 of this guide.

2. After students have heard the dialogue twice, check their comprehension with simple questions that require yes/no or one-word answers. Example: "Should Olga ask her dentist or her obstetrician about taking medicine while she is pregnant?"

3. Students may read the dialogue aloud in groups of three, taking the roles of Olga, Mike, and the nurse and then switching until each student has read each part.

4. Create and conduct pattern drills for greater facility with this pattern:

   Is it safe to _____ during my pregnancy? (exercise, drink beer, work at my job, take aspirin, have sex, go jogging, do aerobics)

Talking It Over (Page 69)

Continue to allow time for stories from your students about their experiences. These are likely to be lively, dramatic, and deeply personal.

Working Together (Page 69)

Students will work in pairs to present arguments for and against having the baby's father present during the delivery. If necessary, suggest reasons such as: "I'm afraid. I'll be so happy when the baby is born, I want him to be there. He can hold my hand." The doctor may counter with, "There's nothing for him to do. He'll be in the way. He'll get sick or faint to see you in pain."

Real Talk (Page 69)

1. The sound of the letters *th* in *thank* is a troublesome sound for new speakers of English. This sound does not exist in most other languages. Point out that the tongue is forward, just behind or between the teeth, and air is released over the tongue. Provide some pocket mirrors so students can see the position of their teeth and tongues as they pronounce the "th" sound.

2. Depending on your students' native languages, the sound of *th* in *thank* may be confused with the "t" or "s" sound. It's worth working on this, since mispronunciation of this phoneme seems comical to some native speakers. A strategy for teaching minimal pairs appears in the **Real Talk** section on pages 54–55 of this guide.

t	th	s	th
tank	thank	sank	thank
tick	thick	sick	thick
tin	thin	sigh	thigh
torn	thorn	sink	think
tree	three	some	thumb

t	th	s	th
bat	bath	mouse	mouth
debt	death	tense	tenth
mat	math	pass	path
wit	with	face	faith
toot	tooth	worse	worth

Putting It Together (Page 70)

1. Draw two stick figures on the board, one taller, thinner (obvious from picture), older (write age, or draw a beard), and richer (put money in one hand) than the other. Elicit comparisons between the two. Point out that when we compare two items, we use a comparative form and the conjunction *than*.

2. Demonstrate the spelling changes of one-syllable adjectives before attaching the suffix *-er*.

   Consonant-vowel-consonant words double the final consonant. Examples are: *big/bigger, fat/fatter, thin/thinner, hot/hotter*.

   Words ending in *e* add only *r*: *wide/wider*.

   Words ending in *y* follow the *y* to *i* rule unless the previous letter is a vowel: *gray/grayer* but *dry/drier*.

3. The *-er* suffix is added to two-syllable adjectives that end in *y* or *le*. Examples are: *happy/happier, funny/funnier, simple/simpler*.

   Other two-syllable words, and all words of three syllables or more, form comparisons with *more* and <u>no</u> suffix: *more handsome, more careful, more thoughtful, more expensive, more beautiful*.

4. When students have practiced comparing two items successfully and can use the forms reliably in speech, present the superlative forms by building on the previous foundation. For instance, teach *thin/thinner/thinnest* and *big/bigger/biggest*. Make sure students understand that when they use the *-est* suffix, they should be comparing more than two items or people.

Read and Think (Page 71)

1. After students use context clues to guess meanings of any unknown words, clarify the meanings through definitions and additional examples.

2. Compare infant mortality rates in the United States today with those in the past or in developing countries today. For example, in the United States, the rate is 13 deaths per 1,000 births, compared to 285 per 1,000 births in Afghanistan and 7 per 1,000 births in Sweden. Ask students what they think are the reasons for the differences in infant mortality rates.

In Your Community (Page 71)

Elicit mothers' experiences with prenatal tests here and in their native countries. Ask, "Did any of you know the sex of your child in advance because of ultrasound testing or amniocentesis? Would you want to know the sex of your child in advance? Why or why not?"

Figuring Out the U.S. (Page 72)

Clarify vocabulary after students have guessed meanings using context clues. Bring in any pictures of hospital delivery rooms or the more modern birthing rooms. Share your own experiences if appropriate.

Your Turn (Page 72)

1. Ask additional questions about childbirth that are appropriate for your students. For example: "In your native country, are women given painkillers during childbirth? Are baby boys routinely circumcised? If so, is that a health measure or a religious act?"

2. Issues such as family planning, birth control, and abortion are likely to be brought up. Exercise particular caution and respect in any discussion of these issues. Some students will find such discussions offensive, while others will wholeheartedly enjoy them. If *you* are uncomfortable talking about these topics, it would be best to avoid them.

12 What's for Supper?

Competency
Responding to questions about a balanced diet

Content Reading
Checking ingredients on food labels

Cultural Reading
Dieting in the United States

Structure
Many/Much

Listening/Speaking Tip
Questions in statement form

Before You Listen (Page 73)

1. Introduce the illustration using the strategies on page 1 of this guide. Ask, "What can you tell about Mike and Olga from their kitchen? When is this scene taking place? Do you think Mike should help cook when his wife is pregnant?"

2. Teach key vocabulary, such as *supper*, *vegetables*, *vitamins*, and *frozen*. Clarify meanings without translating. For example, paraphrase "I don't feel like" with "I'm not in the mood to."

Dialogue (Page 74)

1. Present the dialogue orally, choosing from the strategies on page 1 of this guide.

2. After students have heard the dialogue twice, check their comprehension with simple questions requiring yes/no or one-word answers. Examples: "Did the doctor recommend pizza or fresh vegetables for Olga? Did she say to avoid coffee? Did Olga drink a quart of milk today?"

3. Students may read the dialogue aloud in pairs, taking the roles of Olga and Mike and then switching. Create and conduct pattern practice with the following pattern: I don't feel like _____. (eating, cooking, talking, working, studying English, going out,

washing the dishes) Students can then create new dialogues.

Talking It Over (Page 75)

Ask, "What is tofu?" (soybean curd, a cholesterol-free, low-calorie, inexpensive source of high-quality protein) "What factors decide whether we eat well?" (possible answers: finances, knowledge, planning, available food stores, shopping, season, cooking methods, amount of time to eat) "What other factors affect our meals?" (mealtime conversations, eating alone versus eating with the family, stress)

Working Together (Page 75)

1. Bring in pictures of a variety of foods. Discuss sample daily menus that would include portions from each food group.

2. Plan a health-food party. Have students bring in fruits, vegetables, salads, cheeses, breads, beverages, and selected national dishes. Discuss why each dish is healthy.

Real Talk (Page 75)

Point out the sound changes in informal English when Americans speak quickly. Additional examples include "hafta" (*have to*), "gonna" (*going to*), and "didja" (*did you*).

Putting It Together (Page 76)

1. Gather a number of objects to illustrate both noncountable and countable nouns. Examples: a glass of water, salt in a salt shaker, ink, chalk, catsup, pencils, chairs, books, bananas.

2. Point out that most nouns are objects that can be counted and have singular and plural forms. Review irregular plurals. Explain that other nouns are things that have no distinct size or shape but take the shape of their container: liquids, gases, and grains, for example. Demonstrate by pouring water from one cup into another: anything that can be poured is noncountable.

3. Elicit and write on the board two lists of words: countable nouns and noncountable nouns. Many food items fall in the noncountable category. Some foods fall into both categories: candy, candies; cake, cakes. Animals are countable, but the meat from the animal is noncountable: chickens, chicken; lambs, lamb; turkeys, turkey. Write the plural of the countable forms.

4. Present *a lot of* as a nondefinite counter that may be used with either group, as in this example: I like *a lot of* sugar and *a lot of* raisins in my cereal.

5. Point out that in questions asking about quantity, *how many* is used with countable nouns and *how much* with noncountable nouns.

6. Have students note that *much* as an adjective without *too* is seldom used in affirmative statements, and *a lot of* is the preferred expression. We don't say, "I want much cheese on my pizza" but rather "I want a lot of cheese on my pizza."

7. For *Practice B*, have students work in pairs telling about things they ate or drank too much of at the last party they went to or during the last holiday season. For example: "I drank too much wine. I ate too many cookies."

Read and Think (Page 77)

1. Use the labels from a bread or cereal package to illustrate the nutritional information. A guide to safe and dangerous additives would also be helpful if one is available.

2. Clarify new vocabulary after students have a chance to guess the meanings from the context. Give examples of additives such as sugar, salt, preservatives, food coloring, emulsifiers, wax, and sprays.

3. Discuss the pros and cons of adding preservatives to foods such as breads, cookies, and packaged foods. Ask, "Why do you think apples are coated with wax? Should you peel apples and other fruits before eating them if the fruit has been waxed to keep it fresh?

Should stores be required to have signs listing the sprays, waxes, and colorings added to fresh fruits and vegetables? Are you willing to pay twice the price for foods grown and delivered to market without additives and preservatives?"

In Your Community (Page 77)

1. Make copies of government RDAs for protein, carbohydrates, fat, calories, calcium, fiber, and vitamin C for each student. (A complete RDA chart will also include other vitamins and minerals.)

2. Depending on your students' interests and needs, figure out the calorie count and nutritional values of the junk food they eat and compare with samples of fish, vegetables, rice, and milk.

Figuring Out the U.S. (Page 78)

1. Bring in pictures and advertisements glorifying young and lean bodies. Also bring ads for weight-loss products, low-calorie foods, diet clubs, and health spas.

2. Share your own dieting experiences.

Your Turn (Page 78)

1. Point out that there is a possibility of becoming heavier in the United States if students follow American eating patterns. Sweets are very sweet in the United States, and many foods that are not considered sweet contain sugar. Examples: catsup, frozen dinners, breaded fish sticks, tomato sauce, salad dressing.

2. Ask, "What is the effect of having snacks and candies available at supermarket checkout counters, drugstores, and newsstands?"

Refer to page 62 of this guide for teaching suggestions for Review Unit Four.

Review Unit Teaching Suggestions

The purpose of the review units is to help students develop their communicative competence while reviewing the specific vocabulary and competencies presented in the student text. Each review unit is in the form of a two-page information-gap exercise. Students work in pairs and obtain information orally from their partners in order to complete the task.

To introduce the information-gap exercise, first divide the class into groups A and B. Then match each "Person A" with a "Person B" so that all students are working in pairs. Person A looks only at the first page of the information-gap exercise, while Person B looks only at the second page.

Review Unit One (Pages 19 and 20)

In this activity, students practice making a medical appointment. One student plays a patient, while his or her partner plays a receptionist. Sample questions include: "What are your office hours? Do you have evening hours?" and "Can you come in tonight at 8:30? How is tomorrow night at 7:00?"

The patient must reflect on several possibilities: coming during his or her lunch hour, coming in the morning and going to work late, delegating the parent conference to a spouse, or giving up the bowling activity.

Review Unit Two (Pages 39 and 40)

In this activity, students work in pairs, asking one another questions to discover the differences between two pictures. When they find a difference, they write it down.

Use two students to demonstrate the procedure. Draw two sample stick-figure pictures on separate sheets of paper. In Picture A, a man, a woman, and a girl are walking. The child is wearing a hat. A crescent moon is shining above. Give Picture A to Student A. Let everyone except Student B see the picture.

In Picture B, two men and a girl are walking. The girl is not wearing a hat, and the sun is shining overhead. Let everyone except Student A see the picture.

Students A and B ask each other questions until they discover the three differences. They should write the differences on the blackboard.

Then have students work in pairs to compare the pictures in their texts. Remind students that there are eight differences between the pictures on pages 39 and 40 of the student text. Circulate around the room and listen in on the conversations.

Review Unit Three (Pages 59 and 60)

This exercise reviews vocabulary words from chapters 7–9. Have students work in pairs. Help them understand that each of them has a partly completed crossword puzzle. Students must complete their puzzles by asking their partners for definitions of the missing words. They can ask questions such as: "Tell me about number one across. What is the definition of number one across?"

Definitions should not mention the word. For example, number one across could be defined as follows: "It's the money you get when you work. You have to pay this kind of tax every year." The giver of the definition should allow the other person time to think and should provide further hints if needed: "You need this to spend money and pay your bills. If you don't have this, you are very poor. The word has two parts. The first part is the opposite of *out*, and the second part is the opposite of *go*."

Review Unit Four (Pages 79 and 80)

The purpose of this exercise is to give students practice in reading a simplified chart and comparing the nutritional values of foods. Model the exercise with two students while all books are closed. Then have students open their books and work in pairs to complete the exercise. When students have completed their charts, they take turns making comparisons.

Some students will finish faster than others. Using a nutritional guide, have one of the quicker students write down the nutritional information for tomato juice using the same nutrients that are listed in the chart for orange juice. Students can then compare orange juice with tomato juice, continuing to practice comparative forms. If you like, teach or review the superlative forms to compare orange juice, tomato juice, and the cola drink.

FAMILIES AND SCHOOLS

JANE YEDLIN
AND
CAROLINE T. LINSE

Scope and Sequence

CHAPTER	TOPIC	COMPETENCY
Chapter 1 Don't Worry	Childbirth	Preparing for the birth of a child
Chapter 2 And Baby Makes Three	Child care	Making child-care decisions
Chapter 3 You're Late!	Children's tasks	Understanding different ways to discipline children
Chapter 4 I Might Quit School	Dropping out of school	Understanding the importance of education
Chapter 5 How Old Is Mei?	American schools	Registering a child for school
Chapter 6 You Speak English at Home?	Language	Deciding which language to speak at home
Chapter 7 She Patted Me on the Head	Parental involvement in school	Resolving cross-cultural conflicts at school
Chapter 8 Fire! What Should We Do?	Latchkey children	Reporting an emergency
Chapter 9 I've Got Nothing Better to Do	After-school programs	Selecting quality after-school programs for youth
Chapter 10 Eat What's on Your Plate	Child-rearing practices	Dealing with child-rearing issues
Chapter 11 Domestic Disturbance	Family and the law	Coping with domestic violence
Chapter 12 I Love Being a Doctor	Adult and continuing education	Becoming aware of occupational and educational choices

Families and Schools

CONTENT READING	CULTURAL READING	STRUCTURE
Prenatal care	Childbirth customs	Future with *will/won't*
Different types of daycare	How to choose daycare	Comparatives
Children and discipline	Changes in family life as a result of living in the U.S.	*Supposed to*
Help-wanted ads	Equal educational opportunity for all	*If . . ., can/can't*
American public schools	Teaching styles and discipline in American schools	Wh-questions
ESL and bilingual programs	Benefits of ESL programs	*Used to* (Habitual past)
An elementary school report card	School announcements	Talking about a past event
Emergencies	Safety products for children	*Should/Shouldn't*
After-school programs for teenagers	After-school activities	Reported commands
Special education programs	Attitudes toward youth and parenting	Contrasting *make* and *let*
Children's rights under the law	Ways Americans deal with problems	Conditional sentences
Institutions of higher education	Continuing education for adults	Describing people with *who* clauses

1 Don't Worry

Competency
Preparing for the birth of a child

Content Reading
Prenatal care

Cultural Reading
Childbirth customs

Structure
Future with *will/won't*

Listening/Speaking Tip
-tion/-cian

Before You Listen (Page 1)

1. Introduce the illustration using the strategies on page 1 of this guide.

2. Encourage students to describe the picture. Ask questions such as: "What kind of office is it? How do you think each of the women feels? What is the man doing?" Encourage students to ask their own questions about the picture.

3. Teach key vocabulary such as *pregnant* and *obstetric clinic.*

Dialogue (Page 2)

1. Present the dialogue orally, choosing from the strategies on page 1 of this guide.

2. After students have heard the dialogue twice, check their comprehension with questions such as: "Who is worried about having her baby, Mrs. Chem or Mrs. Santos?"

3. Have students read the dialogue aloud in groups of three, taking the roles of Mrs. Chem, Mrs. Santos, and Mr. Williams and then switching until each student has read each part.

Talking It Over (Page 3)

1. If you have ever prepared for the birth of a child, share your experiences with students. Encourage students to share their experiences. Ask them if their baby was born in the United States or in their native countries and how they think the place of birth may have influenced their experiences.

2. Make a chart on the board similar to the following:

Reasons to Have a Baby in the U.S.	Reasons Not to Have a Baby in the U.S.

Complete the chart with students' answers from questions 1, 2, and 3. Discuss advantages and disadvantages of having a baby in the United States.

Working Together (Page 3)

1. Discuss ways to calm a frightened person. Have students look back at the dialogue for expressions intended to reassure.

2. Write the sample conversation on the board and ask, "What would Mrs. Santos say? How would her friend answer?" Write the conversation the students compose on the board and have them practice it in pairs.

3. After they have mastered the conversation, ask for two volunteers to present it to the class.

4. Encourage students to compose their own conversations based on the one they composed in class. Have students practice them in pairs and present them to the class.

Real Talk (Page 3)

Introduce words that have the "shun" sound written as *-tion* and *-cian*. Explain to students that words that have *-cian* are used to describe what someone does. For example, a musi*cian* refers to someone who plays music, and a pediatri*cian* refers to someone who specializes in pediatrics, the health care of children.

Putting It Together (Page 4)

1. Explain that *will* and *will not* are used to talk about the future. Show students how "I will" can be shortened to "I'll," "you will" to "you'll," etc. The negative of *will* is *will not*. Show students how *will not* can be contracted to form *won't*.

2. *Practice A* should be presented as a listening exercise. Read the dialogue again and have students listen for contractions using *will* or *won't*. Read the dialogue twice, pausing after each sentence for students to write down sentences containing contractions.

3. Explain how hopes for the future may be expressed by using *hope* with a clause containing *will*.

4. Before students begin *Practice B*, make a list of different family members on the board. Discuss with them their hopes for their family members. Write the words they come up with on the board. It may be helpful to make a chart like the one below:

	Family Members	Hopes
I/We hope my	mother son cousin etc.	will stop working will marry a kind woman will be happy etc.

Read and Think (Page 5)

1. Refer to the reading strategies listed on page 3 of this guide.

2. Discuss the reasons behind the health consciousness of pregnant women in this country. Ask students if pregnant women are health conscious in their native countries and how they feel about it.

3. Encourage students to look for caution labels intended for pregnant women on packaging for alcohol, cigarettes, and medicine.

In Your Community (Page 5)

1. Have students go to neighborhood health clinics and gather materials about prenatal care. Whenever possible, have students bring back brochures in English and in their native languages.

2. Bring in childbirth experts and midwives as guest speakers.

3. If students are not able to leave the classroom during this time, bring in pamphlets, brochures, films, or videotapes from local clinics.

4. Be sensitive to any cultural taboos or customs that might restrict men's involvement in the childbirth process.

Figuring Out the U.S. (Page 6)

Share some of the ways babies are named in the United States, such as after a grandparent. Ask students to talk about how names are selected in their native countries.

Your Turn (Page 6)

1. You may wish to discuss local customs and laws related to medical procedures performed on newborns, such as circumcision and ear piercing.

2. Encourage students to talk about how names are selected in their native countries.

3. Have students write down children's folktales from their native countries that explain how babies come. Students may wish to put their stories together to form a multicultural book for children.

2 And Baby Makes Three

Before You Listen (Page 7)

1. Introduce the illustration using strategies on page 1 of this guide.

2. Encourage students to describe what they see in the picture. Ask questions about the picture such as: "What are the people doing? Do you think they are talking or fighting? Why? What do you think the baby would say if she could talk?"

3. Teach key vocabulary such as *daycare center* and *return to work*.

Dialogue (Page 8)

1. Present the dialogue orally, choosing from the strategies on page 1 of this guide.

2. After students have heard the dialogue twice, check their comprehension with questions such as: "Does Mr. Williams want Mrs. Williams to go back to work? Why or why not?"

Talking It Over (Page 9)

1. Ask students how the birth of a child changes people's lives. Encourage students to share their experiences.

2. If you have dealt with daycare issues, share your experiences with students. Encourage students to share their perspectives and experiences.

3. Make a chart with two columns on the board:

Reasons to Go Back to Work	Reasons to Stay Home with the Child

Complete the chart with students' answers from questions 2, 3, 4, and 5 in the student text. Explain to students that in some cases a father, not the mother, will stay at home to take care of the children. Depending upon your students, you may wish to emphasize the advantages of daycare.

Working Together (Page 9)

1. Ask students, "What would a husband say if he didn't want his wife to go back to work? What would a wife say if she wanted to go back to work?"

2. Write the sample conversation on the board and ask, "What would the husband say? How would the wife answer?" Write the conversation students compose on the board and have them practice it in pairs. (Be sure to change pairings, so that each person has the opportunity to work with all the other students in the class.)

3. After they have mastered the conversation, ask for two volunteers to present it to the class.

4. Encourage students to compose their own conversations based on the one they composed in class. Have students practice them in pairs and present them to the class.

Real Talk (Page 9)

First model the rising-falling intonation pattern for a statement such as "I'm going back to work." Then model the rising intonation used to change a statement into a question such as: "Going back to work?" Compare the two types of intonation.

Putting It Together (Page 10)

1. Point out that while "Kiddy Korner" is a catchy name for a daycare center, it is not totally correct. The word *corner* is spelled with a *c*.

2. Explain how comparatives are formed. Adjectives of one syllable can be used as comparisons by adding the ending *-er*. With adjectives of two syllables that end in *-y*, you change the *y* to *i* and add *-er*. The word *more* is added before most adjectives of two or more syllables and *-er* is not used.

3. Students can create a dialogue by completing the exercise. Model the pronunciation in the dialogue for them. Have students practice the dialogue in pairs and then present it to the class.

Read and Think (Page 11)

Before reading about daycare choices, encourage students to share their experience with family home daycare and institutional daycare. Ask parents to describe how their children felt about the experience: Did their children like to go? Did their children talk about what they did at school? Did their children look forward to seeing their friends and their teacher?

In Your Community (Page 11)

Invite institutional and home daycare providers to come and speak to your class. Many daycare centers have rules for parents. Ask the daycare providers to share their expectations for parents, such as keeping children at home when they are ill.

Figuring Out the U.S. (Page 12)

1. Introduce the licensing agencies and government requirements for daycare providers in your area.

2. Discuss the tax credits working parents can receive when they pay for daycare. Check with the IRS for current information.

3. Have students work in small groups and practice asking the questions listed in the second part of the exercise.

Your Turn (Page 12)

1. After discussing the questions, help to arrange for small groups of students to visit local institutional daycare centers and family daycare homes. Have students report back to the class.

2. Have students write a note to a daycare provider. It can describe a real or imagined situation. For example:

March 1

Marissa has a cold. Please give her $1/2$ tsp. of decongestant at noon.

_____
(Signature)

Explain that they should state the problem and what they expect from the daycare provider. They also need to sign the note.

3. Brainstorm for questions students should ask the providers' references. List these on the board. Have students role-play calling and checking references.

4. Although this unit deals with daycare and young children, your students may want to know what services are available for senior citizens who can no longer take care of themselves. Adapt the activities accordingly.

3 You're Late!

```
Competency
Understanding different ways to
discipline children

Content Reading
Children and discipline

Cultural Reading
Changes in family life as a result of
living in the U.S.

Structure
Supposed to

Listening/Speaking Tip
Supposed to/"Spose ta"
```

Before You Listen (Page 13)

1. Introduce the illustration using the strategies on page 1 of this guide.

2. Encourage students to describe what they see in the picture. Ask questions such as: "What could the girl do to make the woman feel less angry?"

3. Teach key vocabulary such as *responsibilities*.

Dialogue (Page 14)

1. Present the dialogue orally, choosing from the strategies on page 1 of this guide.

2. After students have heard the dialogue twice, check their comprehension with questions such as: "What time was Corazon supposed to be home? What was she doing? Is Mrs. Diaz late?"

3. Have students read the dialogue in pairs, taking the roles of Corazon and Mrs. Diaz, and then switching roles so that each student reads each part.

Talking It Over (Page 15)

1. Share conflicts that you or someone you know has had between school or work and family responsibilities.

2. Encourage students to describe conflicts they have had between school or work and family responsibilities. Ask them to tell if and how the conflicts were resolved.

3. List the responses to questions 6 and 7 on the board. As a class, discuss the pressures that single parents face.

Working Together (Page 15)

1. Ask students if they have ever had a conflict with one of their children's teachers. If they have, ask them to talk about how they handled it.

2. Write the sample conversation on the board and ask students, "What would Mrs. Reynolds say? How would Mrs. Diaz answer her?" Write the conversation they compose on the board and have them practice it in pairs.

3. After they have mastered the conversation, ask for two volunteers to present it to the class.

4. Encourage students to compose their own conversations, based on the one they wrote in class. Have students practice them in pairs, and present them to the class.

Real Talk (Page 15)

Introduce "spose ta" as a common pronunciation for *supposed to*.

Putting It Together (Page 16)

1. Explain that *supposed to* is used to express rules. *Not supposed to* is used to express negative rules.

2. Before students do *Practice A* and *Practice B*, have them look back at the illustration on this page and at the dialogue to find Mrs. Diaz's rules for Corazon.

3. Before students do *Practice C*, have them brainstorm for rules they expect their children to follow. Write the rules they suggest on the board. Have them discuss with a partner what children are *supposed to* do and *not supposed to* do.

Read and Think (Page 17)

1. As a pre-reading activity, divide students into small groups. Have each group define and give examples of punishment and/or discipline. Have each group share their responses with classmates. Explain to students that the reading describes a type of discipline used in the United States called *assertive discipline*.

2. Encourage students to ask questions about the three forms of discipline described. Ask them questions to check comprehension, such as: "What is *time out*?" After the class has shown that they understand the reading, ask problem-posing questions such as: "When might you punish a child with *time out*?"

In Your Community (Page 17)

1. Have students address the moral issues related to disciplining children. Ask, "Why do you think child specialists agree that striking or spanking a child is wrong? Are there ever times when it would be all right to strike a child?" Have students explain their answers.

2. Encourage students to discuss the way children are disciplined in their native countries both at home and at school. Ask, "In your country, who do people go to for advice about raising children?"

3. Invite teachers, principals, or child psychologists to come to your class and talk about effective ways to discipline children.

4. Encourage students to discuss how parents and teachers can work together to discipline children.

Figuring Out the U.S. (Page 18)

1. Have students help one another figure out the meanings of unfamiliar words. Discuss different ways to do this.

2. Ask questions to check comprehension, such as: "What has upset Lupe?" or "What is Stanislav's biggest problem in the United States?"

Your Turn (Page 18)

1. Have students form small groups. Each group should write a short informal letter of advice to one of the people on the television talk show. Students should list several possible solutions to each problem.

2. Give students an opportunity to discuss how their lives have changed as a result of moving to the United States. Ask, "What advice would you give someone from your native country who is moving to the United States?"

Refer to page 90 of this guide for teaching suggestions for Review Unit One.

---

4 I Might Quit School

Before You Listen (Page 21)

1. Introduce the illustration using strategies on page 1 of this guide.

2. Encourage students to describe what they see in the picture. Ask, "Who is thinking about quitting school? Does Mr. Williams seem happy about that?"

3. Teach key vocabulary such as *quit school*.

Dialogue (Page 22)

1. Present the dialogue orally, choosing from the strategies on page 1 of this guide.

2. After students have heard the dialogue twice, check their comprehension with questions such as: "Is Bernardo a daytime or a nighttime janitor? Is Bernardo fifteen or sixteen?"

3. Have students read the dialogue in pairs, taking the roles of Mr. Williams and Bernardo, and then switching roles so that each student reads each part.

Talking It Over (Page 23)

1. If you have ever had to decide between school and work, share your experience with students. Discuss how you reached a decision—for example, by making a list of the advantages and disadvantages of each option.

Have students share similar experiences. Discuss the long-term effects of each decision.

2. When students discuss questions 2, 3, 4, and 5, make sure they discuss the short-term and long-term effects of each decision.

Make a chart on the board similar to this one:

Reasons for Bernardo to Stay in School	Reasons for Bernardo to Drop Out of School

Complete the chart with students' answers from questions 2, 3, 4, and 5.

3. Have students write down the items from each of the columns in the chart. Have them work in small groups to put each set of reasons in order from most important to least important.

4. Discuss why mandatory attendance laws were established and how they affect children. Ask, "Why do you think children have to stay in school until they are sixteen? Is this a good law? Why or why not? Do you think this makes them want to stay in school? Why or why not?"

Working Together (Page 23)

1. Discuss negative attitudes that children of all cultures may have toward going to school. Ask, "What can be done so that children want to stay in school?"

2. Write the sample conversation on the board and ask students: "What would Bernardo say? How would Mr. Williams answer him?" Write the conversation they compose on the board and have them practice it in pairs.

3. After they have mastered the conversation, ask for two volunteers to present it to the class.

4. Encourage students to compose their own conversations based on the one they wrote in class. Have students practice them in pairs and present them to the class.

Real Talk (Page 23)

Show how difficult it is to aurally discriminate between *can* and *can't*. Present *can* and *can't* as minimal pairs.

Putting It Together (Page 24)

1. Explain to students that *can* is used to describe things someone is able to do and *can't* is the negative form of *can*.

2. For *Practice A*, ask students, "Which picture shows Bernardo's future if he stays in school? Which one shows his future if he quits school?" Discuss the things that Bernardo and his parents will be able to do depending upon whether or not he drops out of school.

3. Before students begin *Practice B*, brainstorm about decisions they make every day, such as what to cook for dinner. Ask students what the outcome of each action or decision will be. For example, "If I cook chicken for dinner, I can have leftovers for tomorrow night." Encourage students to list several outcomes for each decision.

Read and Think (Page 25)

1. Refer to the reading strategies on page 3 of this guide.

2. Have students find the word *advancement* in two of the want ads. (It is found in the ad for *Data Entry Clerk* and the ad for *Retail Salespersons*.) Have students try to figure out how it is used in each of the ads. Explain the concept of a dead-end job. Discuss which types of jobs in your area are more likely to provide opportunities for advancement.

3. Model the questions students would ask an employer to fill in each column in the job chart. For example, "What are the opportunities for advancement?" Have students work with a partner to role-play a telephone call to a potential employer.

Students may want to write a script to use when they make telephone calls.

In Your Community (Page 25)

1. Elicit the names of occupations that your students are interested in. Write these on the board. Then have students form groups according to the occupations they are interested in. Use local newspaper ads for ideas.

2. Ask students, "How else have you found out about jobs or work?" Students may wish to discuss the importance of *networking* (establishing a group of contacts) when looking for a job.

3. Brainstorm a list of questions a potential employer might ask. Write these on the board. Discuss how to deal with difficult questions such as, "Were you ever fired from a job?" Explain to students that it is illegal for potential employers to ask certain types of questions such as: "Are you married? How old are you?" Talk about how to deal with these questions. Have students work with a partner to role-play a job interview.

4. Brainstorm questions students may want to ask a potential employer. Discuss which ones would be appropriate to ask during a job interview and which ones they should not ask until they are offered a job.

Figuring Out the U.S. (Page 26)

Be sure to spend a few minutes giving students the opportunity to figure out the meanings of unfamiliar words. Ask, "What do you think Dr. King meant by 'content of their character'?"

Your Turn (Page 26)

Students may wish to discuss how to achieve their goals and fulfill their own dreams. Students can work in small groups and brainstorm ways to make their dreams come true.

5 How Old Is Mei?

Competency
Registering a child for school

Content Reading
American public schools

Cultural Reading
Teaching styles and discipline in
American schools

Structure
Wh-questions

Listening/Speaking Tip
Question intonation

Before You Listen (Page 27)

1. Introduce the illustration using the strategies on page 1 of this guide.

2. Show students a public-school registration form from one of the schools in your area. Ask, "If someone wanted to register a child for school, what papers would he or she need?" Encourage students to share experiences they have had registering their children for school.

3. Teach key vocabulary such as *register for school*.

Dialogue (Page 28)

1. Present the dialogue orally, choosing from the strategies on page 1 of this guide.

2. After students have heard the dialogue twice, check their comprehension with questions such as: "How old is Mei? Where does Mrs. Tuy live?"

Talking It Over (Page 29)

1. Discuss how children feel when they have to move or go to a new school. Invite students to share personal experiences.

2. When students talk about questions 1, 2, and 3 of the student text, make sure they discuss Mei's feelings. Ask, "How do you think Mei feels? How do you think Mei will feel if she goes to the elementary school? How do you think she will feel if she goes to the junior high school?"

Make a chart on the board similar to the following:

Reasons for Mei to Attend the Elementary School	Reasons for Mei to Attend the Junior High School

Complete the chart with answers from questions 1, 2, and 3.

Working Together (Page 29)

1. Write the sample conversation on the board and ask, "What would you say? How would Mrs. Feingold answer?" Write the conversation they compose on the board and have students practice it in pairs.

2. After they have mastered the conversation, ask for two volunteers to present it to the class.

3. Encourage students to compose their own conversations based on the one they wrote in class. Have students practice them in pairs and present them to the class.

Real Talk (Page 29)

Model the intonation used to form questions such as: "What's your name? Where do you go to school?"

Putting It Together (Page 30)

1. Explain to students that wh-questions begin with the appropriate question word. Even though *how* does not begin with wh-, it is still considered a wh-question word. Go over the examples in the box for both *to be* and *main verbs*.

2. For *Practice A* ask students, "What do you think Mrs. Feingold asked Mrs. Gonzalez?" After students have completed *Practice A*, have them role-play the dialogue by working with a partner.

3. Before *Practice B*, have them look at the questions they wrote in *Practice A*. Have students make a list of questions they could ask one another. Write their questions on the board. Have students work with partners and practice asking and answering questions. Tell students that if they would rather not give a specific answer, they can reply, "I'd rather not say." Write this response on the board.

Read and Think (Page 31)

1. Refer to the reading strategies listed on page 3 of this guide.

2. Discuss the role of kindergarten in the American public school system. Ask, "Do children in your country attend something similar to kindergarten? Do you think kindergarten is important? Is it better for a child to go to half-day or all-day kindergarten? Why?"

In Your Community (Page 31)

1. Discuss school-placement criteria for elementary, junior high (or middle), and high school students. These include, but are not limited to, location of bilingual and ESL programs, age of children, and spaces available at each school. Have students find out about school placement in your community.

2. In the United States, many public elementary, junior, and senior high schools are required to have parents fill out a form called the Home Language Survey. It is intended to determine if a child comes from a home where a language other than English is spoken. The survey is used to help make sure the students receive bilingual and ESL services. Invite someone from the local public schools to come to your class and discuss how the Home Language Survey helps make sure the Limited English Proficient (LEP) children receive appropriate instruction.

Figuring Out the U.S. (Page 32)

Ask questions to check comprehension and to relate information in the reading to students' own lives. Ask, "Why does Jean-Paul like Mr. Koutz so much? Would Mr. Koutz be considered a good teacher in your native country? Why or why not?"

Your Turn (Page 32)

1. Ask students to write down the name of the best teacher they have ever had. Have them list reasons why they thought the teacher was so good. Have students write a letter similar to the one by Jean-Paul describing their best teacher.

3. Introduce the concept of "Teacher of the Year." Ask students how teachers are honored in their native countries. Have students work in groups and come up with criteria for Teacher of the Year. Have students compare their responses to the ones of their classmates. Their responses could be used to help create or modify teacher evaluation forms.

6 You Speak English at Home?

Competency
Deciding which language to speak at home

Content Reading
ESL and bilingual programs

Cultural Reading
Benefits of ESL programs

Structure
Used to (Habitual past)

Listening/Speaking Tip
Yes/no questions in statement form

Reasons to Speak Your Native Language at Home	Reasons to Speak English at Home

Before You Listen (Page 33)

1. Introduce the illustration using the strategies on page 1 of this guide.

2. Compare the library in the picture to those in your area. Briefly discuss what types of services local libraries provide. Focus on materials available in different languages. Encourage students to ask questions about the picture and to share their experiences.

3. Show students a library card from a local library.

4. Teach key vocabulary such as *bilingual* and *lose a native language*.

Dialogue (Page 34)

1. Present the dialogue choosing from the strategies on page 1 of this guide.

2. After students have heard the dialogue twice, check their comprehension with questions such as: "What language does Mrs. Feingold speak at home? Does Corazon understand much Spanish?"

Talking It Over (Page 35)

1. Make a chart on the board similar to the one in the next column. Complete the chart with students' answers from questions 1, 2, and 3.

2. Have students form small groups. Have each group address one of the following questions:

   - What do you do when a teenager is embarrassed to speak his or her native language in public?

   - Should young children translate for their parents or grandparents? Why or why not?

   - What jobs are available for people who are bilingual?

   Have each group report its findings to the class.

Working Together (Page 35)

1. Write the sample conversation on the board and ask, "What would the student say? How would the librarian answer?" Write the conversation they compose on the board, and have them practice it in pairs.

2. After they have mastered the conversation, ask for two volunteers to present it to the class.

3. Encourage students to compose their own conversations based on the one they wrote in class. Have students practice in pairs and present them to the class.

Real Talk (Page 35)

Model for students statements that are used as yes/no questions, such as: "You like diet soda? You never work late?"

Putting It Together (Page 36)

1. Explain to students that *used to* expresses a past-tense action which no longer exists. The simple form of a verb follows *used to*. *Used to* plus the simple form of a verb expresses the habitual past.

2. For *Practice A*, discuss how Mrs. Feingold's life changed when she came to the United States. Model the language needed: for example, "I *used to* work in a factory."

3. Before students begin *Practice B*, have them discuss their jobs and other activities in their native countries. Write their responses on the board. Have students work in pairs or in small groups and talk about what they *used to* do.

Read and Think (Page 37)

1. Follow the reading strategies on page 3 of this guide.

2. Ask questions to check comprehension and to relate information in the reading to students' own lives. Ask, "What does LEP stand for? What does it mean? Do bilingual programs offer ESL classes? What is the difference between ESL and bilingual programs? Do your children attend ESL classes?"

In Your Community (Page 37)

If possible, conduct a panel similar to the one described in the **Read and Think** section. You may want to include a local teacher, principal, and several parents. Encourage members of the panel to discuss how they help LEP students.

Figuring Out the U.S. (Page 38)

Ask questions to check comprehension and to relate information in the reading to students' own lives. Ask, "Why does James Hsu want to thank the Parents' Advisory Committee? How did the ESL classes help James?"

Your Turn (Page 38)

1. The purpose of the Parents' Advisory Board (PAC) is to help make sure bilingual parents are involved in their children's educations. Translators are provided at PAC meetings. Parents have both a right and a responsibility to be involved in their child's education. This is a very difficult concept for many parents from other countries where this is not the practice. Have your students attend the meeting of a PAC or a similar type of organization. Invite someone who has served on a PAC to come and talk to your class.

2. Discuss the role of parents in American education. Ask, "Are parents encouraged to be involved in education in your native country? Are parents allowed or encouraged to question their local educational programs?"

3. Another option is to invite the director of bilingual education to come to your class and answer questions. You might also wish to arrange a visit to a local bilingual education program.

4. You may wish to invite high school students who have been in bilingual programs to come to your class to share their experiences.

Refer to page 90 of this guide for teaching suggestions for Review Unit Two.

---

7 She Patted Me on the Head

Competency
Resolving cross-cultural conflicts at school

Content Reading
An elementary school report card

Cultural Reading
School announcements

Structure
Talking about a past event

Listening/Speaking Tip
Showing contrast with stress

Before You Listen (Page 41)

1. Introduce the illustration using the strategies on page 1 of this guide. This illustration depicts a cross-cultural conflict. It shows two people with very different perceptions of the same event. Have students discuss the reasons why two individuals might perceive the same situation differently. Reasons include age, gender, and cultural background.

2. Teach key vocabulary such as *customs*.

Dialogue (Page 42)

1. Present the dialogue orally, choosing from the strategies on page 1 of this guide.

2. After students have heard the dialogue twice, check their comprehension with questions such as, "Who is unhappy?"

Talking It Over (Page 43)

1. After discussing the questions, you may wish to do this extension activity: First, have students answer question 5 for their country of origin. Ask students to list gestures used to show approval, disapproval, and surprise.

2. Then have students form groups according to their native countries. Have members of each group share their lists and discuss how customs vary within each country. Encourage students to discuss reasons for variations, such as gender, ethnic background, education

level, social class, and specific geographic locations. Have the group generalize the expressions and gestures in their native countries.

3. Next, draw a chart on the board like the one below. Include countries represented by students in your class. You may want to group the countries according to geographic region, such as Latin America and Asia. Have each group report their responses to the class. Record responses on the chart. Have students compare and contrast similarities and differences.

Countries Represented by Class Members	Gestures Used to Show Approval	Gestures Used to Show Disapproval	Gestures Used to Show Surprise
Thailand			
Mexico			
Japan			
Samoa			
Chile			

4. Finally, students may use their responses for question 7 of **Talking It Over** to create a booklet or handout for U.S. teachers and school personnel. This booklet could be entitled *"Cross-Cultural Awareness: Helpful Hints for Teachers."*

Working Together (Page 43)

1. Write the sample conversation on the board and ask, "What would Mr. Chem say? How would Mrs. Williams answer?" Remind students that they may use the answers to questions 7 and 8 of **Talking It Over** to help them write the conversation. Write the conversation they compose on the board and have them practice in pairs.

2. After students have mastered the conversation, ask for two volunteers to present it to the class.

3. Encourage students to compose their own conversations based on the one they wrote in class. Have students practice them in pairs and present them to the class.

Real Talk (Page 43)

Model the way words are stressed to show a contrast or difference in meaning. *I'm sorry. Mrs. Reilly LIKES Phon very much.*

Putting It Together (Page 44)

1. Explain that you add *-ed* to a regular verb to make it past tense. Have students practice the rule with examples such as *talk, ask, listen,* and *laugh.* Sometimes the last letter is doubled, as in *pat, drop,* and *pet.* (This rule is applied to one-syllable verbs that end in a single consonant except *c, h, w, x,* and *y* and are preceded by a single vowel.) Go over the examples for irregular past-tense verbs.

2. Refer students to the Appendix on page 83 for a list of past tense forms of the irregular verbs.

3. To help students memorize the past forms of irregular verbs, play the game "Team Tic-Tac-Toe." See page 2 of this guide for an explanation.

4. For *Practice A,* have students use the illustration to answer the questions about the parent-teacher meeting. (The answer to question 6 can vary.)

5. Before students begin *Practice B,* have them brainstorm misunderstood customs. Have students describe what happened. Write their responses on the board using the past tense. Have students work in pairs or in small groups and talk about what they used to do.

Read and Think (Page 45)

1. Discuss the way the school year is divided. There are usually four grading periods.

2. After discussing the questions in the **Read and Think** section, discuss the situation from different perspectives. Ask, "If you were Mrs. Tuy, what would you ask Chanta? If you were Chanta, how would you answer?" Write their responses on the board. Have students work with a partner and create a dialogue.

3. Invite several teachers who grade students differently to come to your class. The teachers can explain how they assign grades.

4. Parent-teacher conferences help parents learn about their child's performance in school. Not all parents take advantage of this opportunity. Remind parents that they may request a translator for parent-teacher conferences. As a class, brainstorm questions for parents to ask teachers; for example: "What are my son's strengths? What can I do at home to help my daughter?"

In Your Community (Page 45)

1. Collect report cards from local schools. Be sure to include samples of different grade levels. Have students compare and contrast them.

2. Ask students to describe the grading systems used in their native countries. Also ask students what they as parents should do when a teacher grades too strictly or is too "easy" on students.

Figuring Out the U.S. (Page 46)

Ask questions to check comprehension and to relate information in the reading to students' own lives. For example, ask, "How can adult family members get involved at Jefferson School? What opportunities are available at your children's schools for you to become involved?"

Your Turn (Page 46)

1. Give students an opportunity to share their parenting skills. Ask questions such as: "What do you do with a teenager who hates to study? How do you teach your children the importance of school?"

2. Bring in or have students bring in school newsletters. The newsletter from Jefferson School shows that the school encourages parent involvement. Ask students, "What can you learn about your elementary school from its newsletter? Does the newsletter only list sports events? Does the newsletter invite parents to attend school functions?"

8 Fire! What Should We Do?

> **Competency**
> Reporting an emergency
>
> **Content Reading**
> Emergencies
>
> **Cultural Reading**
> Safety products for children
>
> **Structure**
> *Should/Shouldn't*
>
> **Listening/Speaking Tip**
> Oral spelling

Before You Listen (Page 47)

1. Introduce the illustration using the strategies on page 1 of this guide. Ask questions such as: "What should the children do? Should they try to put out the fire? Should they call for help first?"

2. Teach key vocabulary such as *should* and *shouldn't*.

Dialogue (Page 48)

1. Present the dialogue orally, choosing from the strategies on page 1 of this guide.

2. After students have heard the dialogue twice, check their comprehension with questions such as: "Who wants to cook dinner? Who wants to wait until their mother gets home?"

Talking It Over (Page 49)

1. While discussing the questions, be sure to address the issue of supervision for school-age children. Point out that it is a major problem facing parents in the United States. (Chapter 9 will follow up with various after-school activities and programs.) Discuss the problems caused when children are left alone or expected to baby-sit. Ask questions such as: "How old should a child be before he or she is left alone? How old should a child be to baby-sit?"

2. Talk about smoke detectors, fire alarm boxes, fire escape routes, and ways to put out small fires.

3. Teach your students the **Stop, Drop, and Roll** steps used to put out a fire on their clothing. Schools and parents teach children what to do in case their clothes are on fire: they are to **stop** what they are doing, **drop** to the ground, and **roll** to smother the flames.

Working Together (Page 49)

1. Provide students with an opportunity to share their experiences with emergencies. Ask, "What happened? What did you do? Did you call for help?" You might want students to reenact conversations they had with emergency personnel. (This might be a sensitive subject for some students, so use discretion.)

2. Write the first sample conversation on the board and ask students, "What would the person at the fire department ask? How would Sasha answer?"

3. After they have mastered the conversation, ask for two volunteers to present it to the class.

4. Encourage students to compose their own conversations, based on the ones they wrote in class. Have students practice them in pairs and present them to the class.

5. Repeat steps 1–3 for the second dialogue.

Real Talk (Page 49)

Show students how names can be spelled easily. Use simple words to clarify which letter they are referring to. *Regules* would be spelled *R* as in *rabbit*, *E* as in *egg*, *G* as in *gum*, etc. Have students work with partners and practice spelling their own names while their partners write what they say.

Putting It Together (Page 50)

1. *Should* is used to describe an obligation to do something. If you *should* do something, then you need to do it.

2. For *Practice A*, have students use the illustration to describe what the children *should* and *shouldn't* do.

3. Before students begin *Practice B*, have the class brainstorm things they should do to make their homes safer.

Read and Think (Page 51)

1. Find out the procedures used in your area to access emergency services. These are usually listed in a special section of the telephone book. Find out if you have 911 or enhanced 911 service. (When a caller uses enhanced 911 service, the caller's address and telephone number appear on the emergency operator's screen. The operator is able to send help even if the caller can't give the correct address.)

2. Present the emergency procedures used in your community. Telephone companies, fire departments, and police departments often provide pamphlets that tell people what to do in case of emergencies. These are often available in languages other than English.

In Your Community (Page 51)

1. Go over the emergency information chart with students. Discuss the reasons why it is necessary to have each piece of information written down before an emergency happens. Explain to students that doctors often ask for children's birth dates before they begin treatment.

2. Role-play other emergency situations. Have students practice calling for and asking for help. Talk about the need to have someone who is able to translate into one's native language.

3. Invite someone from a local emergency agency to speak to your class. Ask them to talk about what to do in case of an emergency. They may also discuss emergencies that are common in your area, such as earthquakes, tornadoes, or hurricanes.

Figuring Out the U.S. (Page 52)

Ask questions to check comprehension and to relate information in the reading to students' own lives. Ask questions such as: "What does *childproof* mean? Why do outlets need covers?"

Your Turn (Page 52)

1. After going over the questions in the student text, discuss ways to teach children to stay away from dangerous household products. Contact your local poison-control center for free "Mr. Yuck" stickers and child safety pamphlets. The stickers show an unhappy face. Parents can peel them off and place them on dangerous products.

2. Before doing the writing activity, discuss situations or products that are especially dangerous for children. Then, have students work in small groups to write a law or design or modify an existing product. For example, if the dangerous situation has to do with poisonous household products, they may want to write a law requiring all dangerous products to have childproof caps.

9 I've Got Nothing Better to Do

> **Competency**
> Selecting quality after-school programs for youth
>
> **Content Reading**
> After-school programs for teenagers
>
> **Cultural Reading**
> After-school activities
>
> **Structure**
> Reported commands
>
> **Listening/Speaking Tip**
> *Hanging out*/"Hangin' out"

Before You Listen (Page 53)

1. Introduce the illustration using the strategies on page 1 of this guide. Encourage students to share their impressions of the place in the picture. Ask questions such as: "Do you think the arcade is a safe place? Would you want to go there late at night? Would you let your children go there? If they really wanted to go there, could you stop them?"

2. Teach key vocabulary such as *wasting your time*.

Dialogue (Page 54)

1. Present the dialogue orally, choosing from the strategies on page 1 of this guide.

2. After students have heard the dialogue twice, check their comprehension with questions such as: "Who is playing a video game, Luis or Bernardo?"

Talking It Over (Page 55)

1. While discussing the questions, talk about the problems caused when teenagers do not feel good about themselves or have productive ways to spend their time. Ask, "How can you tell if your teenager is having problems? What can you do if your teenager doesn't feel good about himself or herself? How can you improve communication between you and your teenager?"

2. Address the complex issue of finding productive activities that teenagers want to do. Have students locate schools and agencies that offer activities for teenagers after school and during vacations.

3. Another option is to talk about how involved parents should be in the lives of their teenagers. Ask, "What rules do you have for teenage boys? Do you have different rules for teenage girls? Should parents tell teenagers who they can have as friends?"

Working Together (Page 55)

1. Write the sample conversation on the board and ask students, "What would Arturo say? How would Bernardo answer?" Remind students that they may use the answers to questions 2, 3, and 5 of **Talking It Over** to help them write the conversation. Write the conversation they compose on the board and have them practice in pairs.

2. After they have mastered the conversation, ask for two volunteers to present it to the class.

3. Encourage students to compose their own conversations based on the one they wrote in class. Have students practice them in pairs and present them to the class.

Real Talk (Page 55)

Model the way verbs ending in *-ing* are often pronounced in informal conversation, for example, *talking* -> "talkin' ," *eating* -> "eatin' ." Explain that although this is the way they are pronounced, they are spelled with the full *-ing* ending.

Putting It Together (Page 56)

1. Explain to students that when you report a command, you use *told* and then change the command to the *to + verb* form. When students want to report a negative command, they use *not + to + verb*. You may want to give some examples from your class by asking your students, "What did I tell you to do for homework?" "You told us to do *Practice A* on page 45."

2. For *Practice A*, have students look at each of the illustrations and identify who is telling whom what to do.

3. Before students begin *Practice B*, have them brainstorm things they have told others to do. They should also brainstorm things they have been told to do. Write these on the board. Encourage students to refer to them as they complete *Practice B*.

Read and Think (Page 57)

1. Refer to the reading strategies listed on page 3 of this guide.

2. Ask questions to check comprehension and to relate the reading to students' own lives, such as: "Why do so many places offer programs for teenagers?"

In Your Community (Page 57)

1. Make a chart on the board with these heads:

Organization	Activity	Age	Boys/Girls	Cost

Have students use pamphlets and brochures they have collected to complete as much of the chart as possible. Students may then make telephone calls or visit each program to complete the chart. Have students compare and contrast the purposes of each of the programs offered. (Students should be wary of some religious groups that offer programs for teenagers. Some of these programs are designed to "convert" teenagers.)

2. Explain to students that in the United States, it is very common for boys and girls to attend school and after-school activities together. (However, there are some exceptions to this such as Boy Scouts and Girl Scouts.) Ask students if girls and boys are grouped together or separated for school and after-school activities. Discuss the pros and cons of each system.

3. Have students visit and compare after-school programs for teenagers. Encourage students to ask teenagers what they like and dislike about each program.

4. If students may not leave your class during class time, invite speakers to talk to your class. Representatives from agencies offering after-school programs as well as school counselors and members of youth organizations would be appropriate.

Figuring Out the U.S. (Page 58)

This reading shows how individual teenagers were able to find constructive, culturally appropriate activities in the United States. Illustrate this point by making a chart on the board like this one:

Teenager	Home Country	U.S.
Laura	Mexico	Helps get ready for Mexican-American Celebration

Your Turn (Page 58)

1. If possible, invite teenagers to come to your class and talk about problems they face. Select teenagers who are doing well in school as well as those who have overcome problems such as alcohol abuse, depression, or poor grades. Encourage them to talk about how they spend their time and how they feel about themselves. You might also want them to describe an ideal parent.

2. Discuss special problems teenagers have when their families move from one country to another. Talk about ways to cope with these problems.

> **Refer to page 90 of this guide for teaching suggestions for Review Unit Three.**

10 Eat What's on Your Plate

> **Competency**
> Dealing with child-rearing issues
>
> **Content Reading**
> Special education programs
>
> **Cultural Reading**
> Attitudes toward youth and parenting
>
> **Structure**
> Contrasting *make* and *let*
>
> **Listening/Speaking Tip**
> Using *always/never* for emphasis

Before You Listen (Page 61)

1. Introduce the illustration using the strategies on page 1 of this guide. Encourage students to tell you their impressions of Sasha's behavior. Ask, "Why do you think Sasha is making that face? What would you do if Sasha were your son?"

2. Teach key vocabulary such as *annual banquet* and *yuck*.

Dialogue (Page 62)

1. Present the dialogue orally, choosing from the strategies on page 1 of this guide.

2. After students have heard the dialogue twice, check their comprehension with questions such as, "Why isn't Sasha eating his dinner?"

Talking It Over (Page 63)

1. Before discussing the questions, introduce the words *strict* and *lenient*. Discuss different approaches to parenting and youth. Brainstorm the advantages and disadvantages of each approach.

2. Ask students if their parents were strict or lenient. Ask them to give examples, such as: "My father was very strict. He made me come home by 9:00 every night." Make a chart on the board like the one in the next column. Have students copy the chart and write down the way they were treated as children.

Students should then write down if they are going to parent their children the same way or differently.

Ways I Was Parented	Ways I Parent or Will Parent
My father made me come home very early every night.	I make my daughters come home very early every night.

Have students form small groups. Discuss how the way they were parented affects the way they behave as parents.

Working Together (Page 63)

1. Write the sample conversation on the board and ask students, "What would Mr. Feingold say? How would Sasha answer?" Remind students that they may use the answers to questions 2 and 3 of **Talking It Over** to help them write the conversations. Write the conversation they compose on the board and have them practice in pairs.

2. After they have mastered the conversation, ask for two volunteers to present it to the class.

3. Encourage students to compose their own conversations based on the one they wrote in class. Have students practice them in pairs and present them to the class.

Real Talk (Page 63)

Model the way *always* and *never* are used for emphasis.

My parents *always* made me eat breakfast.

My parents *never* made me go to bed early.

Putting It Together (Page 64)

1. Explain that when you force someone to do something you *make* them do it. *Let* is used when you allow someone to do something.

2. For *Practice A*, ask students, "Who is strict—Mr. or Mrs. Wong? Who is lenient—Mr. or Mrs. Wong?"

3. Before students begin *Practice B*, have them brainstorm instructions they give to baby-sitters. After students have completed the dialogue, group them in pairs. Ask them to role-play the dialogue they have completed.

Read and Think (Page 65)

1. Refer to the reading strategies listed on page 3 of this guide.

2. Ask questions to check comprehension and to relate the reading to students' own lives. Some examples are: "Why did Mrs. Lee call Mr. Berlin? How does the school test children who are bilingual?"

In Your Community (Page 65)

1. Have students visit special education classes. You might want to invite a special education teacher to talk to your class. Special education teachers can explain how they help children with special needs or educational handicaps.

2. Another option is to have your class discuss the stigma parents and students sometimes feel when they receive special education services. This could be compared with the feelings of frustration students have when they have trouble learning.

Figuring Out the U.S. (Page 66)

Answer key: 1. D; 2. E; 3. B; 4. C; 5. F; 6. A

Your Turn (Page 66)

1. As an extension activity, have students work in small groups: group members should select or make up a saying that best describes how they feel about parenting. Students in each group will need to make compromises in order to come to an agreement.

2. Another activity is to bring in articles from parenting magazines that deal with problems parents face. Problems you may wish to include are toilet training, children who resist going to bed, and children who hate to do their homework. Have students work in small groups and offer solutions to each problem. Students could write up their answers.

11 Domestic Disturbance

Competency
Coping with domestic violence

Content Reading
Children's rights under the law

Cultural Reading
Ways Americans deal with problems

Structure
Conditional sentences

Listening/Speaking Tip
Conversation fillers

Before You Listen (Page 67)

1. Introduce the illustration using the strategies on page 1 of this guide. Encourage students to tell you how they view police officers in the United States and in their native countries. Ask students, "Can you trust the police in your native country? Why or why not? Can you trust the police in the United States? Why or why not?"

2. Draw the following family tree on the board.

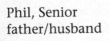

Phil, Senior   Sally
father/husband   mother/wife

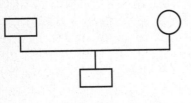

Phil, Junior
son

Discuss words that show relationships, such as *father* and *husband*, as well as the differences between *junior* and *senior*. Explain to students that *Sr.* is used as an abbreviation for *senior* and *Jr.* is used for *junior*.

Dialogue (Page 68)

1. Present the dialogue orally, choosing from the strategies on page 1 of this guide.

2. After students have heard the dialogue twice, check their comprehension with questions such as, "Is this the first time the police have been called to 1433 West Broadway?"

Talking It Over (Page 69)

1. Write the word *help* on the chalkboard. Ask students what they think it means. Discuss how the meaning varies based on the context. *Help* needed to make a cake is very different from *help* needed to overcome a drinking problem.

2. Because of the personal nature of this subject, students should not be required to take part in this discussion if they would rather not. Have students form small groups. Have each group select three or four questions they would like to answer. It is all right if all of the groups select the same questions. The groups should share their responses with the entire class. With such a sensitive topic, it is more important that students feel comfortable participating in the discussion than it is for all of the content to be covered.

Working Together (Page 69)

1. Address the issue of help for Phil and Phil, Jr. Ask students, "What kind of help does Phil need? What kind of help does Phil, Jr., need?" Write their responses on the board for students to refer to as they compose the role play.

2. Write the following conversation on the board:

Aunt Phyllis: Junior, are you OK?

Phil, Jr.:   I guess so.

Aunt Phyllis: What's wrong?

Phil, Jr.:   Well, it's my dad. I love him a lot. But he scares me.

Aunt Phyllis:

Phil, Jr.:

Ask students, "What would Aunt Phyllis say? How would Phil, Jr., answer?" Write the conversation they compose on the board.

3. Write the following conversation on the board:

Aunt Phyllis:	I don't know how to tell you this.
Phil, Sr.:	Tell me what?
Aunt Phyllis:	I'm really worried.
Phil, Sr.:	
Aunt Phyllis:	

Write the second conversation they compose on the board. Have students practice both conversations in groups of three.

4. Encourage students to compose their own conversations based on the ones they wrote in class. Have students practice them in pairs and present them to the class.

5. After they have mastered the conversation, have two volunteers present it to the class.

Real Talk (Page 69)

Model the way *hmm* and *well* are used to fill a pause in the conversation. Give examples such as:

"Well, [pause] I don't know what I'm going to do."

Putting It Together (Page 70)

1. Explain to students that conditional sentences with *if* and *would* are used to talk about what you would do if you were in someone else's place (or shoes).

2. For *Practice A*, model the language needed: "If I were Sally, I would be scared."

3. Before students begin *Practice B*, have each of them list the names of three or four of their friends or relatives. Have students think about how their friends or relatives could improve their lives. Model a sentence for them:

"If I were Aunt Margaret, I would take my medicine every day."

Read and Think (Page 71)

Allow students to select which questions they would like to answer. Encourage but don't force students to share personal experiences.

In Your Community (Page 71)

Discuss the meaning of the phrase *safe place*. Ask, "What would make a place safe for an abused child, or an abused wife?"

Figuring Out the U.S. (Page 72)

1. Mention that when people write letters to advice columnists, they don't usually use their real name.

2. Ask questions to check comprehension and to relate information in the reading to students' own lives.

Your Turn (Page 72)

1. As a class, have students brainstorm advice they would give to Suzanne. Have them work in small groups and write letters of advice to Suzanne. Remind students they may use their answers to question 3.

2. Bring in advice columns from newspapers. You may want to include columns that offer advice for personal problems. Have students work in small groups. Give each group a problem from the newspaper. Do not include the accompanying advice. Have each group write a letter of advice in response to the problem. After the group shares its letter with the class, read the advice that was given in the newspaper.

12 I Love Being a Doctor

> **Competency**
> Becoming aware of occupational and educational choices
>
> **Content Reading**
> Institutions of higher education
>
> **Cultural Reading**
> Continuing education for adults
>
> **Structure**
> Describing people with *who* clauses
>
> **Listening/Speaking Tip**
> Interrupting

Before You Listen (Page 73)

1. Introduce the illustration using the strategies on page 1 of this guide.

2. Encourage students to talk about the way the woman in the picture is dressed. Students can ask you yes/no questions to figure out what Semra Bashar did in her native country.

3. Explain the names of the tests that are on the bulletin board in the illustration. GMAT stands for Graduate Management Admissions Test, GRE stands for Graduate Record Exam, MCAT stands for Medical College Admission Test, and FMGEMS stands for Foreign Medical Graduate Exam for Medical Schools.

4. Teach key vocabulary such as *practice medicine*.

Dialogue (Page 74)

1. Present the dialogue orally, choosing from the strategies on page 1 of this guide.

2. After students have heard the dialogue twice, check their comprehension with questions such as, "What was Semra Bashar's occupation in Turkey?"

Talking It Over (Page 75)

Before discussing the questions, help students understand the importance of academic and career counseling. Explain that Mr. Fournier answers many different questions about jobs. Ask, "What questions could Mr. Fournier answer? What questions do you think he would be unable to answer?" Write these on the board.

Working Together (Page 75)

1. Make a chart on the board:

	Law	Education	Medicine
Require More Education/ Experience	*Judge*	*College president*	*Physician*
Require Less Education/ Experience	*Security guard*	*Teacher's aide*	*Nurse's aide*

As a class, discuss the experience and education that would be required for each job in the United States as well as in the students' native countries.

2. Write the following conversation on the board:

> Mr. Fournier: May I help you?
> Mr. Camacho: Yes, in my country I was a . . .
> Mr. Fournier:
> Mr. Camacho:

Ask students, "How would Mr. Camacho finish the sentence? How would Mr. Fournier answer?" Write the conversation they compose on the board. Have students work in pairs and practice the conversations.

3. Encourage students to compose their own conversations based on the one they wrote in class. Have students practice them in pairs and present them to the class.

4. After they have mastered the conversation, ask for two volunteers to present it to the class.

Real Talk (Page 75)

Sometimes Americans interrupt the speaker to "help" the speaker finish a sentence. Although this may seem rude, they are often sympathizing with the speaker.

Putting It Together (Page 76)

1. Students will need to refer to earlier chapters of the book to complete *Practice A*. There is no one right answer for any question.

   (1) Mr. Fournier is found in Chapter 12.

   (2) Sally is found in Chapter 11.

   (3) Corazon is found in Chapter 3.

   (4) Bernardo is found in Chapters 4 and 9.

   (5) Mr. Williams is found in Chapters 1, 2, and 4.

   (6) Mrs. Santos is found in Chapter 1.

   (7) Mrs. Feingold is found in Chapters 5 and 6.

   (8) Phon is found in Chapter 7.

2. Before doing *Practice B*, have each student pick the names of two to three other students in the class. Explain that they are to write several sentences about each of the people they chose. Have students share these with their classmates.

Read and Think (Page 77)

Ask questions to check comprehension and to relate information in the reading to students' own lives. Ask, "Can you get a Ph.D. at a community college? Where do you think you could go to get an A.A. degree? What local schools offer B.A. degrees?"

In Your Community (Page 77)

1. Have students work in small groups and research a specific local college or a university. Urge students to visit the college or university. Students may make group reports to the rest of the class about the institution they chose.

2. Invite admissions officers and guidance counselors from local colleges to speak to your class.

Figuring Out the U.S. (Page 78)

Ask questions to check comprehension and to relate information in the reading to students' own lives.

Your Turn (Page 78)

1. Encourage students to discuss their hopes and plans for the future.

2. Create a class yearbook. Students may wish to give awards to their classmates: funniest, friendliest, or most frequent traveler, for example.

> Refer to page 90 of this guide for teaching suggestions for Review Unit Four.

Review Unit Teaching Suggestions

The purpose of the review units is to help students develop their communicative competence while reviewing the specific vocabulary and competencies presented in the student text. Each review unit is in the form of a two-page information-gap exercise. Students work in pairs and obtain information orally from their partners in order to complete their task.

To introduce the information-gap exercise, first divide the class into groups A and B. Then match each "Person A" with a "Person B," so that all students are working in pairs. Person A looks only at the first page of the information-gap exercise, while Person B looks only at the second page.

Review Unit One (Pages 19 and 20)

Be sure students understand that each of them has a partly completed map of the setting where the story of *Families and Schools* unfolds. Familiar places such as the Obstetric Clinic from Chapter 1 and the Child Development Center from Chapter 2 are identified on either of the two maps. The students' task is to complete their maps by asking their partners directions to the buildings that are not identified on their own maps. Before students begin, elicit some helpful expressions and write them on the board; for example, "Where is Jefferson School? How do I get to Kiddy Korner? Go two blocks, then turn left on Adams Street."

Review Unit Two (Pages 39 and 40)

This acrostic puzzle features vocabulary from Chapters 4–6. Students may refer to the Index on pages 85–86. In this case Person A and Person B have the same puzzle, but Person A's has the sentences that will help guess the odd-numbered words, and Person B's has the sentences that will help guess the even-numbered words. Only by working together can the students complete their task. (The hidden message is "Education Pays.")

Review Unit Three (Pages 59 and 60)

This puzzle describes several situations similar to the emergency situation in Chapter 8. Because some of the vocabulary may be new to the students, be sure to go over the emergency vocabulary first.

Person A and Person B have the same puzzle, but Person A's has the sentences that will help guess the odd-numbered words, and Person B's has the sentences that will help guess the even-numbered words. (The hidden message is "Help! Emergency!")

After working together to complete their puzzle, each pair of students could choose one of the emergency situations and write a role play about what they would do in case of that emergency.

Review Unit Four (Pages 79 and 80)

The final review unit covers the vocabulary from Chapters 1–12. If necessary, students may refer to the Index on pages 85–86. Person A and Person B each have three brief stories with underlined words and subscripts that refer to the write-on lines. Person B has the list of expressions for Person A's stories, and vice versa. Students work with their partners to decide which expressions match the underlined expressions in their stories and then write those expressions in the blanks provided.

Contemporary's
Choices
An ESL Lifeskills Series for Adults

This series develops the critical language skills, knowledge base, and problem-solving abilities ESL students need to participate actively in U.S. society. These dynamic competency-based texts help students make informed choices about consumer options, health care, and parenting and schools.

Program Components

- Consumer Sense
- In Good Health
- Families and Schools
- Teacher's Guide

Teacher's Guide

The *Choices Teacher's Guide* expands the versatility of the *Choices* series. This guide includes general teaching suggestions for *Consumer Sense*, *In Good Health*, and *Families and Schools* as well as step-by-step instructions for the preparation and presentation of each lesson.

Special Features

- Helpful teaching strategies
- Scope-and-sequence charts
- Easily identifiable goals and topics
- Page-by-page teaching suggestions

CB
CONTEMPORARY
BOOKS

180 North Michigan Avenue
Chicago, Illinois 60601
(312) 782-9181

ISBN: 0-8092-4045-9

CHOICES
AN ESL LIFESKILLS SERIES FOR ADULTS
IT'S YOUR RIGHT

JOHN CHAPMAN

RIDGEWATER COLLEGE
Hutchinson Campus
2 Century Ave SE
Hutchinson MN 55350-3183